Searchlights for Spelling
Year 4 Teacher's Book

Chris Buckton   Pie Corbett

Contents

CAMBRIDGE
UNIVERSITY PRESS

CAMBRIDGE UNIVERSITY PRESS
Cambridge, New York, Melbourne, Madrid, Cape Town, Singapore, São Paulo, Delhi

Cambridge University Press
The Edinburgh Building, Cambridge CB2 8RU, UK

www.cambridge.org
Information on this title: www.cambridge.org/9780521891806

First published 2002
4th printing 2007

Printed in the United Kingdom by Polestar Wheatons

A catalogue record for this publication is available from the British Library

ISBN 978-0-521-89180-6 paperback

ACKNOWLEDGEMENTS
The publishers would like to thank the following
for helping with the trialling of *Searchlights for Spelling*:

Abbotsmead Junior School, Cumbria
Ashbrook First School, Milton Keynes
Braniel Primary School, Belfast
High Bentham CP School, N. Yorks
Manorbrook Primary School, Bristol
St Richard's RC Primary School, Chichester
Watton-at-Stone Primary School, Herts

Barrow Community Learning Partnership (EAZ), Cumbria

Illustrations by Cecilia Johansson, Priscilla Lamont, Ian Newsham and Rachel Merriman.
Cover background photograph of coral reef: Kelvin Aitken/A.N.T./NHPA
(Natural History Photographic Agency)

Design and layout by Pentacor plc.

Searchlights for Spelling

Searchlights for Spelling is a comprehensive spelling scheme for Years 2–6/Primary 3–7 that covers all the word-level spelling objectives of the National Literacy Strategy (NLS), meets the requirements of the National Curriculum and supports the English curricular requirements of Scotland, Wales and Northern Ireland.

It is a systematic scheme for teaching the patterns of the English spelling system through stimulating, multi-sensory activities. It builds up spelling concepts through an investigative approach, equipping children with the skills to tackle new words as well as developing their strategies for the recall of key words and spelling patterns.

The scheme also builds on NLS programmes such as Progression in Phonics (PIPs) and Spelling Bank and is cross-referenced to them, making use of their basic interactive techniques such as 'Get Up and Go', 'Show Me', and 'Time Out' (see Key terms, page 4 for further explanation).

Spelling for writing

The reason for learning to spell is to become fluent in everyday writing. *Searchlights* is designed to equip children to write fluently, rather than simply to learn and be tested upon decontextualised lists of words. It aims to make spelling enjoyable, through developing a sense of curiosity about words and an awareness of language patterns.

The sessions begin by deepening children's *understanding* of an objective or strategy, through direct teaching or investigation. This is followed by *applying* their understanding through shared writing and independent activities. It is important to ensure that spelling objectives are always emphasised in the children's own writing, in order to reinforce the concept of spelling for a purpose.

A multi-sensory approach

The activities are based on four key learning styles:

visual – remembering common patterns; writing words down to check whether they 'look' right; looking at the 'tricky' bit and trying the letters in a different order; looking for words within words; seeing the word in your mind, holding a word in your memory by seeing it, then looking to the top left of your mind to recall it.

aural and oral – hearing and pronouncing words; emphasising or exaggerating pronunciation to aid learning (e.g. *Wed-nes-day*); breaking words into syllables or phonemes; remembering some words with a rhythmic strategy (e.g. *Mrs d, Mrs i, Mr ffi, Mr c, Mr u, Mrs lty: difficulty*); using rhyme to spell by analogy.

kinaesthetic – writing common patterns; tracing over words; sky-writing as you say each letter; getting the feel of common handwriting joins.

cognitive – knowing rules, conventions, possible and impossible combinations; identifying word roots, suffixes and prefixes; using knowledge of grammar (e.g. ed – past tense), using mnemonics (e.g. *there is a rat in separate*).

By experiencing a multi-sensory teaching approach, children who learn in different ways have every chance of developing their ability to spell. Good spellers use a range of strategies. The whole-class and pupil activities use a variety of approaches. To further support multi-sensory teaching, the above symbols are given next to the quickfire activities for each unit – Oddbods and Snip-snaps (see Key terms, page 4).

Identifying and representing phonemes

Searchlights generally follows the NLS framework conventions for identifying and representing phonemes, including the use of 'long' and 'short' to distinguish certain vowel sounds. For the most part, *Searchlights* adopts other NLS terminology. Phonemes are represented by bold type in all materials, while letter patterns are red in the Teacher's Book, Big Book and Pupil's Book and underlined in the Photocopy Masters Book.

It is important to note that the teaching of certain phonemes and their associated letter patterns can be affected by regional variation in pronunciation. You will need to adapt your teaching of these phonemes to suit the needs of your class. Such instances are noted in the relevant units.

Spelling practice – little and often

Children need frequent practice so that spelling becomes automatic and does not interfere with the act of composition. *Searchlights* is designed to be as flexible as possible and can be used in a variety of ways, depending on the needs of the children. The activities fit naturally into word-level work within the literacy hour and have a simple, regular pattern. They can be adapted for different classes and groups.

Spelling and handwriting

Searchlights emphasises the important link between spelling and handwriting, particularly in Year 4. Regular practice of handwriting joins helps to consolidate the learning of common letter strings. A joined script is offered wherever it is intended that a child will copy or continue the writing.

Spelling log

It is helpful for children to develop the habit of keeping a personal spelling log. It can contain:

- collections of words arising from the independent activities;
- lists of oddbods (see Key terms below) and other 'tricky' words;
- results of spelling investigations;
- dictations and other tests;
- personal spelling targets;
- useful strategies or mnemonics;
- space for **Look Say Cover Write Check** practice.

A possible format for a spelling log is included in the Photocopy Masters Book for those who want to make use of it. Reference pages in the Pupil's Book and extra pages in the Big Book also provide useful material which the children could transfer to their log.

How to use *Searchlights for Spelling*

Key terms

Brush-ups:	activities which revisit objectives from the previous year, for those children who need more time to catch up.
Catch-you-out:	a word that is an exception to a specific rule or teaching point (e.g. where a word changes completely when forming a plural rather than just adding s or es).
Get Up and Go:	individual children come out to the front to demonstrate something.
Oddbod:	a 'tricky' word that causes common difficulties (featured on the Big Book left-hand page and in the list of words to learn in each unit).
Show Me/Time Out:	all children can respond by writing on dry-wipe boards and showing the spelling attempt.
Sky-writing:	drawing the shape of a letter or word in the air as an aid to memory.
Snip-snaps:	short, snappy ideas for further practice in applying the unit's objective or in learning key words.
Spelling log:	a personal ongoing record of words being learnt – (see Photocopy Masters Book page 13).
Think about ... / Extra challenge:	both these suggestions take the children a little further in exploring or applying a spelling concept.

Colour-coding

Red type is used to highlight target letters and letter patterns. To highlight phonemes and distinguish them from spelling patterns, they are printed in bold type.
(In the Photocopy Masters Book, where colour is not used, letters and letter patterns are underlined and phonemes are in bold.)

The components

For each year there are four key components:

- **Teacher's Book** – containing a double-page spread of step-by-step notes for each unit's teaching as well as background information.
- **Big Book** (or **OHTs** for Years 5–6/Primary 6–7) – containing a double-page spread of whole-class material for each unit as well as useful revision and supporting material.
- **Pupil's Book** – containing a double-page spread of differentiated activities for each unit as well as reference pages with word lists and reminders of spelling rules and strategies.
- **Photocopy Masters Book** – containing a photocopiable homework copymaster (PCM) for each unit as well as revision activities, assessment material and guidance for parents.

Together these resources provide 18 core units of work for the year (six units a term). Three additional units provide further material, which can be fitted in as necessary. Each unit comprises two parts:

- Part 1 – introduces the spelling objective(s).
- Part 2 – takes the objective(s) one step further, or introduces a further objective, and provides a test dictation.

Part 1

Teaching the objective(s): Swift, lively interactive teaching of objective(s), using the left-hand page of the Big Book, plus teaching of key words, including 'oddbods' (see Key terms).

Using the objective(s): Developing the skill or concept through writing, including brief opportunities for shared writing.

Independent work (Pupil's Book): Differentiated activities focusing on reinforcement and extension of target objectives (see Differentiation, following). This may take place as part of a literacy hour, or at another time.

Review (plenary): Review of independent work and recap of main teaching points.

Homework: Reinforcement task, generally with investigative element which can involve other family members; words to learn for the unit's dictation.

Part 2

An extended whole-class session.

Teaching the objective(s): Revisiting and developing the unit focus, using the right-hand page of the Big Book.

Using the objective(s): Writing with the class, pausing and discussing spelling points.

Review (plenary): Review and summary of new learning, and discussion of homework findings.

Follow-up homework: This allows for further exploration or reinforcement of learning.

Test dictation: Class dictation that includes examples of the spelling objective and oddbod(s) for the week.

Differentiation

Independent activities in the Pupil's Book are differentiated at three levels, A, B and C. A and B activities consolidate children's learning of the key objectives of the unit, while C activities are more challenging or address a further objective. C activities may anticipate Part 2. Children could work through all three when appropriate. The Extra Challenge in some units extends children's learning further.

Children who find spelling particularly difficult may need extra time to revisit key objectives from the previous year or years. *Searchlights* also provides a bank of Brush-up ideas based on the previous year's objectives as well as six extra revision PCMs.

For each unit, the words to learn list on the homework PCM is differentiated so that some children can be given fewer target words to learn.

Paired spelling

Children could spend ten minutes every day following this simple procedure in order to learn their individual lists (between five and ten words at a time). This procedure could also be introduced to parents and it is given as part of the 'How to help your child with spelling' guidance (see Photocopy Masters Book, pages 47–8).

- The child reads the word; says it aloud; spells the letters out; tries to spell it out without looking.
- Together, parent/partner and child discuss 'tricky bits' and devise a way of remembering them.

■ If the child finds the word hard to remember, repeat the first two stages as necessary before attempting to write.
■ The spelling partner/parent covers the word.
■ The child writes it down.
■ Together they check – if incorrect, revisit two or three more times.

Assessment

The units include a dictation test, as well as a termly SATs-style test to track progress. To be useful, spelling tests should always be diagnostic. Look carefully at the results to find out what strategies the children are using. It is important, too, not to penalise them for incorrect but intelligent, plausible guesses. One useful approach is to allocate two marks to each word: the first mark could be given if the target phoneme, pattern or rule is correct (e.g. *ai* spelt correctly in *rain*) and the second if the whole word is correct.

A simple Tracking sheet to help you monitor children's progress is provided in the Photocopy Masters Book (page 3). Children's involvement in assessing their own progress in spelling is very important. To encourage children to review their own learning, yearly self-assessment sheets with 'I can' targets are also provided (see Photocopy Masters Book, page 14).

Test dictation

The object of regular dictation is to give the children practice in spelling words in context, reinforcing the importance of accurate spelling in writing.

Searchlights dictation provides three levels of differentiated sentences for each unit. The children learn the words before they are tested on some of them in context. In Year 4/Primary 5 there are fifteen words to learn per unit: comprising words related to the unit's objective(s) (wherever possible words are drawn from the NLS list of medium frequency words) and the oddbod(s).

Test scores and comments can be recorded on the teacher Tracking sheet (see Photocopy Masters Book pages 3–5). The suggested procedure for the test dictation is as follows.

Introduction (first unit)
■ Explain to the children what a dictation is.
■ Tell them that you will be dictating sentences.

Procedure
■ Tell them that first, you'll read the whole sentence while they listen. Specify whether you want them to write out the whole sentence or just the target words.
■ Then explain that you'll read a little bit at a time while they write it down (if they are writing the whole sentence).
■ Tell them what to do if they come to a word they don't know: try to break the word up into its sounds, or think of another rhyming word which perhaps they can remember how to spell.
■ Give prompts where appropriate, e.g. reminding them of rules or asking questions such as: *Remember that oddbod? Listen to that word again – what sound can you hear?*
■ Read each sentence through again so that they can check their writing.
■ Note: Make sure that you do not expose strugglers. Children should simply write the words they have learnt (A, A/B, A/BC). There is no need to draw attention to differences here.

Homework

For each unit, a homework PCM provides the related list of words to learn and a task that reinforces the unit's teaching, or focuses on revision. The sheets also encourage an investigative approach. Words to learn for each unit are offered in three levels of difficulty. They are referred to as key words in the Photocopy Masters Book and listed there in full on page 6.

Parents/carers are offered further guidance on a separate PCM: 'How to help your child with spelling'.

Scope and sequence chart – Year 4

Unit	NLS Objectives	Big Book	Pupil's Book	Homework PCM	Snip-snaps	Oddbods
1 Double consonants	NLS 4.1.W5	Long/short vowel sounds; Double/single consonants	Cloze activities with double consonants; Finding more double consonant words	Alphabet doubles	Syllable Fingers Quick-fire Spelling Find a Rhyme	stopped
2 Investigating homophones	NLS 4.1.W6	Investigating homophones in riddles	Choosing the correct homophone spelling	Beat the riddler	Homophone Pairs Hear the Homophone Quick-fire: there, they're or their?	their there they're
3 Verb endings	NLS 4.1.W7	Spelling verb endings	Removing ing and spelling root correctly Adding ing, s and ed to root words	Change ends!	Rhyming Pairs All Change Add the End	asked
4 Irregular tense changes	NLS 4.1.W8	Spelling irregular tense changes	Matching past and present tense; Changing present into past tense	Then and now	Past and Present Change the y Pick the Past Tense	think thought
5 Suffixes al, ary and ic	NLS 4.1.W9	Spelling suffixes al, ary and ic; Identifying root words	Changing nouns into adjectives with al and ic; Adjective riddles	Personal wordsearch	Key Word Speed Writing Thumbs Up or Down	told
6 Using suffixes to change word class	NLS 4.1.W14	Using suffixes to make verbs from nouns/adjectives, nouns from verbs	Making verbs from nouns and adjectives; Adding suffixes ate, en, ify, ise	Specialise in suffixes!	Choose the Suffix Key Word Basketball Verbs into Nouns	change
7 Adding suffixes	NLS 4.1.W9	Adding suffixes	Adding the suffixes ment or ness; Adding the suffix ish	Adding suffixes	Word Building Ron and Ern Key Word Challenge	being
8 Adding suffixes to words ending in f – plurals	NLS 4.2.W5	Adding a suffix to words ending in f – making plurals	Plurals of words ending in f; Changing plurals to singular and vice versa	Half and half	Word Association Plural to Singular Riddles Game	half
9 Common word endings	NLS 4.2.W6	To spell words with the common endings ight, ious, ial, ough, ion	Choosing the correct spelling: ight or ite; Brainstorming ight and ough words	Call it a day!	Quick Rhyme Got Enough? Reveal	might
10 Prefixes al, ad and af	NLS 4.2.W7	Spelling prefixes that use a	Words with al and ad prefixes	Class rules!	All Change! Words Within a Word Plus Word Endings	any
11 Prefix roundup	NLS 4.2.W7, W8	Common prefixes: what do they mean?	Adding prefixes un, over, pre, post, sub and inter	Prefix word wheel	Dictionary Chase Prefix Pelmanism Key Word Sort	until

Scope and sequence chart – Year 4 cont.

Unit	NLS Objectives	Big Book	Pupil's Book	Homework PCM	Snip-snaps	Oddbods
12 Letter strings w + vowel, ss	NLS 4.2.W4, W8; 4.3.W5	Letter strings wa, ss	Finding words with letter strings wi, wo and wa	Warbling words	Letter String Link Hiss and Miss Key Word Sentence Race	guess
13 Investigating k, v and l	NLS 4.3.W3, 4, 5	Kicking k, consonant v	k at beginning, middle and end of the word	Investigating letter strings with l	Letter Hunt Fish and Chips a and b Key Words	across
14 Same spelling, different pronunciation	NLS 4.3.W6	Matching letter strings which do not rhyme	Same spelling, different pronunciation: ow, ou, ough	gh investigation	i before e except after c Investigation String-along Tens (or fives) Quick-fire Quiz	though
15 Common roots	NLS 4.3.W7	Meanings of roots, word webs	Identifying roots and their meanings; Finding and using words with common roots	Look for the Latin	Number Roots Pressure Point Beetle	sure
16 Suffix roundup	NLS 4.3.W8	Suffixes and their meanings	Making adverbs from adjectives; Making adjectives from verbs by adding ful or ive; Making nouns from verbs by adding ure or ment	Automatic adjectives?	Add-on Ants Suffix-stuffed Sentences Word Shapes	different
17 Suffixes ible, able and ion	NLS 4.3.W3, W4, W9	Adding ible or able, tion or sion	Sorting ible and able; Adding ible and able to roots; Making nouns from verbs by adding tion or sion	Test your family or friends!	Show Me Wipe-out Key Word Soccer	suddenly
18 Diminutives	NLS 4.3.W12	Suffixes and prefixes; small and big synonyms	Prefixes/suffixes meaning 'small'; Making words with prefixes or suffixes	Huge homework	Nickname Investigation Make-your-own Diminutives Key Word Roundup	under
Additional 1 Spelling strategies	NLS 4.3.W1, W2, W3	Error analysis; spelling strategies	Finding spelling errors; Analysing spelling errors; Finding words with similar spelling pattern	Spelling questionnaire	Regional Differences Swap Shop Key Word Sort	other
Additional 2 Making adjectives	NLS 4.3.W3, W8	Making adjectives from nouns and verbs	Making adjectives from nouns and verbs with suffixes	Spot the change	Verb, Noun, Adjective s or z Investigation Some Compounds	electricity
Additional 3 Contractions	NLS 4.3.W10	Using apostrophes	Changing full forms to contractions and vice versa; Sorting apostrophes into contraction and possession	Contraction Snap	Contraction Snap Short Cuts Key Word Sentence Race	don't

YEAR	TEACHER RESOURCE	WHOLE-CLASS TEACHING	PUPIL RESOURCE	HOMEWORK REINFORCEMENT ASSESSMENT
Y2	Teacher's Book	Big Book	Pupil's Book	Copymasters
Y3	Teacher's Book	Big Book	Pupil's Book	Copymasters
Y4	Teacher's Book	Big Book	Pupil's Book	Copymasters
Y5	Teacher's Book	OHTs	Pupil's Book	Copymasters
Y6	Teacher's Book	OHTs	Pupil's Book	Copymasters

9

1 Double consonants

Part 1 | You need

Big Book page 2; dry-wipe boards or notebooks; Pupil's Book pages 2–3; PCM 1

Whole class

- To introduce the objective, clap out one- and two-syllable words (e.g. *jam, flat, shopping, battle, spot, tug, running, supper, pop, mummy, daddy*). Children put thumbs up when they hear two syllables.
- Focus on the BBk page. Ask the children to suggest ways of sorting the words on the page.
- Once the words are sorted into two lists, ask what the difference in spelling is. What is the difference in the way the vowel sounds?
- Do they remember the rule about doubling consonants when adding suffixes like ing? Can they see a similar pattern here?
- Generate a rule, e.g. in two-syllable words, if the vowel in the first syllable is 'long' then use one consonant (*biter*); if it is 'short', use two consonants (*bitter*).
- Introduce the oddbod: *stopped* – see below.
- Write some sentences together that combine single- and double-consonant words from the BBk, e.g. *The rider was ridding himself of fleas. Far below I heard a bellow*.
- Tell children about the catch-you-out *modern* (mod words are exceptions to the doubling rule, e.g. *model, modest, module*).

Pupil activities

A and B: Decide whether or not to double the consonant.
C: List double consonant words and make up puzzle sentences.

Extra challenge: Make a list of letters that never double.

Review

- Recap: double the letter after a 'short' vowel in the first syllable of a word, e.g. *grab – grabbing*.

Homework

Make an alphabet of two-syllable words with double consonants.

Oddbod   stopped
- Revisit the rule for doubling consonants after a 'short' vowel sound, and link it to *hop/hope* and the past tense *hopped/hoped*.
- Ask: what is the most common ending for verbs in the past tense such as *rushed, hunted, jumped*? (ed)
- Write up *stopt, stoped* and *stopped* – which looks right? Which is most likely?
- Rhyme the past tense with *hop – hopped, shop – shopped, flop – flopped, mop – mopped, pop – popped, top – topped*.

Snip-snap   Syllable Fingers
- Call out words, e.g. *began, didn't, walk, think, told, jumping, opened*.
- The children hold up one, two, three or more fingers, depending on the number of syllables. Remind them that if they say the word quietly with a hand on their chin, each syllable makes the chin drop.

NLS objective for Unit 1

4.1.W5

Part 2 | You need   Big Book page 3; dry-wipe boards or notebooks

Whole class
- Quickly revisit the previous session on doubling the consonant after the 'short' vowel sound.
- Focus on the BBk page.
- Ask children to come up and complete each rhyming couplet, using the words at the bottom of the page.
- The children think of further rhyming pairs (prompt if you need to, e.g. ask them to find a rhyme for *swallow, mellow, hilly, scribble, bobble, bitter*).
- Together, invent more couplets using the same pattern.
- Discuss spelling in the course of writing.

Review
- Recap on the rule for two-syllable words: double the consonant after a 'short' vowel sound in the first syllable.
- Talk about catch-you-outs (h, q, v, w, x) that do not double; mod words are another exception.

- Homework review.
- Discuss words children found and check spellings.

Follow-up homework
- Write down the rule and exceptions, giving several examples.

Test dictation
- OB Bad weather stopped the football match.
  A   The brown rabbit was hopping round the garden.
      My father said that I must not be silly.
  B   My friends all love my new puppy.
      A hippo is not as large as an elephant.
  C   "I'm sorry that I can't come on Sunday," said Joy.

Snip-snap   Quick-fire Spelling
- Call out a word with a double consonant. You could use animals (e.g. *rabbit, puppy, kitten, otter, hippo, doggy, cattle*).
- Children spell the word on dry-wipe boards, scoring a point for correct spelling.

Snip-snap   Find a Rhyme
- Say a word with a double consonant.
- In pairs, children think of a rhyme and write it down. Score one point for a word no-one else has thought of.

2 Investigating homophones

Objectives for Unit 2

To distinguish between the spelling and meanings of common homophones

Part 1

You need Big Book page 4; dry-wipe boards or notebooks;
Pupil's Book pages 4–5; PCM 2

Whole class
- Explain the term *homophone* – a word which sounds the same as another word but has a different meaning and spelling, e.g. *there*, *their* and *they're*. Compare with *homonym* (from Y3 term 3) – a word with the same spelling but a different meaning to another word.
- Focus on the BBk page. Work out the riddles together (*hare/hair*, *tale/tail*, *hole/whole*, *bear/bare*, *beach/beech*).
- Show how context helps you know which word (and so spelling) is intended.
- Discuss ways to remember the different spellings, e.g. chant 'y-o-u spells you'.
- Brainstorm some more homophones, e.g. *stare/stair*, *bee/be*, *knew/new*, *heard/herd*, *peace/piece*.
- Talk about the few common homophones that it is easy to muddle, e.g. *your/you're*, *to/two/too*, and also the oddbods *their/there/they're* (you could introduce them here – see below).
- Write some sentences together, combining homophones, e.g. *They're going there tomorrow with their teacher. I knew it was new. I heard a herd of cows.*

Pupil activities
A: Choose the correct homophone spelling.
B and C: Replace incorrect homophone spellings.

Think about ...: Putting homophones in your spelling log.

Review
Recap on words that don't change and words that drop the final e when adding ing.

Homework
Solve homophone riddles.

Oddbods their, there, they're
- *They're* is easy enough. (Can you say *they are* instead?) Apply the rule for apostrophe in place of missing letters.
- The problem is distinguishing between *there* and *their*.
  - *their* means 'belonging to';
  - *there* is related to *here* and shows *where* something is, e.g. it is over *there* (and not *here*).

Snip-snap Homophone Pairs 👁💬✍
- Write up a homophone (e.g. *pair*).
- Children write down the alternative spelling (e.g. *pear*).
- If some struggle, offer a clue, e.g. *I bought a pair of juicy ...*
- Try: *be* (*bee*), *knew* (*new*), *right* (*write*), *threw* (*through*), *whole* (*hole*), *sea* (*see*), *know* (*no*), *eye* (*I*), *for* (*four*).

NLS objective for Unit 2
4.1.W6

Part 2 | **You need**   Big Book page 5; dry-wipe boards or notebooks

Whole class
- Quickly revisit the previous session on homophones.
- Focus on the BBk page. Look at the first two riddles together (you could cover up the homophones each time so that children have to solve the riddles themselves).
- Make up new homophone riddles together, using the words given.

Review
- Re-emphasise the importance of context for understanding which word (and so spelling) is required.
- Discuss helpful ways to remember the different spellings.

- Homework review.
- Discuss answers to the riddles. Ask any children who made their own riddles to share them with the class.

Follow-up homework
Make a list of any common homophones that you muddle up when writing. Think of ways to remember them (e.g. mnemonics).

Test dictation
OB The children left all of their carrots.
A   A hare is like a big rabbit.
    The bus fare to town is one pound.
B   My sister and I often go swimming in the sea.
    The sleepy kitten opened one eye.
C   I threw the ball into the garden next door.

Snip-snap   Hear the Homophone
- Write on the board both words from a homophone pair (e.g. *be* and *bee*).
- Say a sentence that includes one of the words. (e.g. *The bee stung me*)
- Children write down the spelling they think is correct.
- Try common homophones from the NLS high frequency word list (see Spelling Bank page 22).

Snip-snap   Quick-fire – *there, they're* or *their*?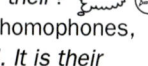
- Say a sentence using one of the three homophones, e.g. *There is a horse. They're feeling ill. It is their horse, not mine.*
- Children write the word *there, they're* or *their* on dry-wipe boards.
- Remind them of the importance of context:
  – *their* – is it 'belonging' to someone, so is followed by an adjective or noun?
  – *they're* – can it be replaced by *they are*?
  – *there* – is it a place word? Does it go with *are* or *is*?

3 Verb endings

<table>
<tr><td>Objective for Unit 3
To spell regular verb endings</td></tr>
</table>

Part 1

You need   Big Book page 6; dry-wipe boards or notebooks; Pupil's Book pages 6–7; PCM 3

Whole class
- Focus on the BBk page. Look at each picture in turn and ask the children what is happening.
- Write the root verb under each picture (*skip, jump, skate, clap, smile, walk*).
- Get Up and Go: ask individuals to turn the verb into s, ing and ed forms. Talk about tense as well as what has happened to the root verb each time, e.g. *The dog jumps / is jumping / jumped*.
- Who knows or can work out the two rules? Use red pens to underline endings and make alterations clear.
- Write up more examples of base form verbs and s, ing and ed forms on the board.
- Write sentences together to practise applying the rules, e.g. *Mum saw her jumping. The earth was moving.*
- Introduce the oddbod: *asked* – see below.

Pupil activities
A: Word subtraction – take away ing and spell the root.
B: Word addition – add ing and ed to a root.
C: Write a poem using lots of verbs with ing, s and ed endings.

Extra challenge: Investigate doubling consonants when adding ed ending.

Review
- When you add ing on to a verb:
  - if the verb ends in e, remember to remove the e, e.g. *move – moving*;
  - if the verb has a 'short' vowel before a single final consonant then double the consonant, e.g. *tip – tipping*.

Homework   Spell verbs with s, ed and ing endings to accompany pictures.

Oddbod   asked
- This can cause problems for children who pronounce it 'arsked'.
- Make a rhyming list, e.g. *ask, bask, cask, flask, mask, task*.
- Use swift joining to gain the feel of the spelling.
- Chant 'a-s-k'.

Snip-snap   Rhyming Pairs
- Say a verb, e.g. *winning*.
- Children write down a rhyming word, e.g. *spinning*.
- If they struggle, give a clue.
- Include some verbs that end in e, e.g. *hating* (*skating*), *making* (*shaking*).

NLS objective for Unit 3

4.1.W7

Part 2 | You need   Big Book page 7; dry-wipe boards or notebooks

Whole class
- Quickly revisit the previous session on removing the e and doubling consonants when adding ing.
- Focus on the BBk page. Work through the investigation to find out if the same applies to past tense (ed) and present (s).
- Get Up and Go: children complete the chart.
- Discuss whether the same rules apply throughout.
- Write a few sentences using some of the words on the chart, contrasting past and present, e.g. *Yesterday, she hoped to go swimming. Today, she hopes to go again.*

Review
- Most words just add s, but those that end in a hissing or buzzing sound (e.g. sh, ss, x) add es, which helps with pronunciation.
- Words that end in e, drop the e when adding ing and just take the d of ed (to avoid doubling the e).
- One-syllable words with a single 'short' vowel before the final single consonant, double the final consonant. One way to remember this is to think of 111 (rather than 999), i.e. one syllable, one 'short' vowel, one consonant = double consonant!
- Words ending in consonant + y, change y to i and add es or ed, but keep y when adding ing (to avoid double i).

- Homework review.
- Discuss the results of the homework, asking children to say which rule they're using each time.

Follow-up homework
Write the basic rules in your spelling log and then note down any verbs that behave differently as preparation for the next unit.

Test dictation
OB I asked Mum if I could have a baby rabbit.
A   The happy hippo was walking by the sea.
     Dad was watching us through the window.
B   The fast cars were racing round the town.
     John rested for a while by the sea.
C   She sipped the cool, clear water.

Snip-snap   All Change
- Focus on verbs in the key word list, e.g. *ask, watch, show, start, use, turn, jump, walk.*
- Write up a verb (e.g. *watch*) plus some optional endings, e.g. *s, es, ing, ed.*
- Say the word with one of the endings, e.g. *watched.* Children write it on dry-wipe boards.
- Then say 'all change' and say the word with a different ending. Again, everyone writes it.

Snip-snap   Add the End
- Focus on an ending, e.g. *ed.*
- Say a root word, e.g. *stop.*
- Pairs of children write the word, adding the ending, on dry-wipe boards.
- Score a point for each correct spelling.

4 Irregular tense changes

Objective for Unit 4

Spelling irregular tense changes

Part 1 | **You need** | Big Book page 8; dry-wipe boards or notebooks; Pupil's Book pages 8–9; PCM 4

Whole class
- Focus pupils on the BBk page. Read through the baby talk and discuss what we normally say, e.g. *I went*, not *I goed*. Circle the incorrect verbs.
- Show Me: children write the correct spellings on dry-wipe boards.
- Can the children suggest other examples that follow the same spelling patterns? (e.g. *bring/bought*, *fight/fought*, *buy/bought* – see Spelling Bank list, page 24.)
- Introduce the oddbods *think* and *thought* and link them to *bring/bought*, etc.
- Write a short story together, using as many irregular verbs as possible. Give an opening sentence, e.g. *The penguin strode down the street.* Then continue together, e.g. *It came into our classroom and told us a story, then wrote a message for our teacher and rode off in a sports car.*

Pupil activities
A: Match present and past tense spellings.
B: Transform a poem from present to past tense.
C: Transform a passage from present to past tense.

Extra challenge: Find past tense catch-you-outs.

Review
- Some verbs have irregular past tense endings. These have to be learned. It's helpful to keep a note in spelling logs to refer to.
- Start a classroom collection of irregularities. Encourage the children to notice them in speech, shared reading and their own writing.

Homework
- Write past and present tense sentences to compare 'when I was a baby' with now.

Oddbods think, thought
- Think is th plus ink. Make up a mnemonic, e.g. *when you write, you think in ink*.
- *Thought* is related to *think* so it starts th – the hard bit is ought. Remember this by writing it quickly to get the feel, chanting the letters rhythmically, visualizing it and making a note in spelling logs.
- List other words with the ought pattern, e.g. *brought, bought*.

Snip-snap Past and Present
- Together, write sentences contrasting past and present. Start by offering a model, e.g. *Long ago people thought that children should be seen and not heard but now we see and hear children very clearly!*
- Try: *Last year ... but this year ...*; *Millions of years ago ... but more recently ...*

NLS objective for Unit 4

4.1.W8

Part 2 | You need   Big Book page 9; dry-wipe boards or notebooks

Whole class
- Focus on the BBk page. Read through the account in the present tense.
- Circle the verbs on a second reading.
- Show Me: pick out the verbs and ask children to write the past tense spelling for each one on their dry-wipe boards.
- Get Up and Go: invite volunteers to write the verb in its present and then past tense form on the chart.

Review
- Not all verbs in the past tense end in ed. Some change their spelling considerably. It does help to say the word and use this as a memory jog. Write it, read back what you have written, and look at it. Does it look right? Use other tricks, such as simple mnemonics.

- Homework review.
- Ask children to share some of their sentences with the class.

Follow-up homework
- Keep a list in your spelling log of any past tense words that you often need and find it hard to spell. Refer to the list whenever you get stuck.

Test dictation
OB   I thought the otter in the sea looked happy.
A   The little boy began to pat the puppy.
     Last term we swam at school.
B   Bill wrote such a funny story at school today.
     Jane and Ben ate four fish from the sea.
C   Dad drove to town and did the shopping.

Snip-snap   Change the y
- Revisit what happens to verbs that end in y when put into the past tense.
- Say a verb in the present tense form (e.g. *cry*); children all say the past tense (*cried*).
- Use *try, spy, try, fry, multiply, apply, hurry, terrify, accompany, worry*.
- Ask the children to formulate a basic rule, e.g. if y has a consonant before it, then change to i (e.g. *cry – cried*).
- Try catch-you-out *fly* (*flew*). It is easy to remember because you do not say 'I flied'!

Snip-snap   Pick the Past Tense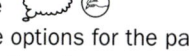
- Say a verb, e.g. *I fall*. Then give options for the past tense, e.g. *I felled* or *I flew* or *I flewed*.
- Children put their thumbs up for the one that sounds right.
- Children then write a sentence on their dry-wipe boards that includes the past tense form.

5 Suffixes al, ary and ic

<table>
<tr><td colspan="2">

Objective for Unit 5

To recognise and spell suffixes al, ary and ic
</td></tr>
</table>

Part 1 | You need

Big Book page 10; dry-wipe boards or notebooks; Pupil's Book pages 10–11; PCM 5

Whole class

- Focus on the BBk page and read the poem through together.
- Get Up and Go: children identify and circle the words ending in al, ary and ic.
- Can they identify what word class they all belong to? (adjectives) Point out that these adjectives are all formed from nouns or verbs.
- Can they identify the root word each time? Demonstrate with the first example: *acrobatic = acrobat + ic.*
- On dry-wipe boards, children continue to write down the root words in the poem, e.g. *atom, exception, sensation, imagine* (note that the e drops), *rhythm.*
- Brainstorm lists of other words with similar endings. Start with adjectives but then extend to nouns (see Spelling Bank list, page 25).
- Note that as these are vowel suffixes, root words may drop a final e or change y to i, and that al often follows on (e.g. *sensational*).
- Note that it is easy to muddle ery, ary and ory. (But it is easy to remember that *history = his story*.)
- Write some sentences together, using the lists, e.g. *The traffic is stationary. Go to the library to find some traditional tales. The queen's anniversary is a national holiday.*
- Introduce the oddbod: *told* – see below.

Pupil activities

A: Change nouns into adjectives by adding al.
B: Add suffixes al or ic to nouns and complete a passage.
   (Answer: exceptional/national/historic/musical/traditional/ occasional/vocals/sensational)
C: Answer riddles and invent some more.

Extra challenge: Find the root words.

Review

- al, ary and ic are vowel suffixes. Added to root nouns and verbs they can form adjectives.
- Some nouns have the same endings (e.g. *hospital, dictionary, music*).

Homework

Make a wordsearch for al, ic and ary words. Give it to someone at home or school to complete.

Oddbod   told

- Usually, past tense words end in ed. So is it: *I tell – I telled*?
- Link to earlier work on irregular past tense verb forms (Unit 4).
- List rhyming words for *told*, e.g. *cold, bold, hold, old.*
- Make up a mnemonic, e.g. *I told you I was old.*

Snip-snap   Key Word

- Select words from the Y4 term 1 medium frequency word list (page 62 of the NLS).
- Call out words for the children to spell, vary the instruction to keep the different strategies in mind, e.g. Who can spell out loud … ? Who can write down … ? Who can sky write (and say) … ? Listen, is this the way to spell … ?

Part 2 | **You need**   Big Book page 11; dry-wipe boards or notebooks

Whole class
- Remind children of the work last session on suffixes al, ary, ic.
- Read the signs and phrases on the BBk page. Discuss their meanings and where they might be found.
- Focus on the adjectives. Children jot down the root words on dry-wipe boards. Check and circle in the BBk. Discuss how the spelling may alter when a suffix is added.
- Pause at *special* and *dental*. The roots are not obvious: *special* is ultimately from the Latin *species*; *dental* is from the Latin *dens/dentis*, meaning 'tooth'.
- Write short sentences using two or three of the words in each, e.g. *The hospital has many special departments.*
- Look at the noun *rehearsal*. What verb does it come from? (*rehearse*) Highlight the dropping of the e and recap on the rule for adding a vowel suffix.
- Similarly, focus on *historical* to recap on the rule y changes to i. Link it to *historic* and compare meanings (*historic* = special/important in history).

Review
- Recap the rules: root words drop a final e or change y to i when adding a vowel suffix; al often follows on (e.g. *sensational*, *exceptional*).
- To remember spelling it can help to exaggerate pronunciation of endings, e.g. *Feb-ru-ary.*

- Homework review.
- Ask the children to swap their wordsearches with a partner.

Follow-up homework

Get used to remembering common words, such as *January* and *February*, by remembering the ary ending and using over-pronunciation or mnemonics such as *Angry Rabbits Yatter.*

Test dictation

OB   My mother told me not to be silly.
A   The musical boy sang a song for us.
     At Christmas we eat traditional food.
B   On the first of January it was cold and wet.
     The church in our town is very historic.
C   Unfortunately Jim is unwell and is in hospital.

Snip-snap   Speed Writing
- Speed-write *told*: how many times in 30 seconds?
- Say a root word. Children write the root plus al.
- Try the following: *season, nation, sensation, person, music, globe, fate, rehearse.*

Snip-snap   Thumbs Up or Down
- Say a word ending in the **ic** sound. Children put their thumbs up if it ends in ic and down if it ends in ick.
- Mix up single-syllable words (*trick, sick, slick, brick, kick, flick*) with multi-syllabic words (*panic, tropic, specific, historic*).
- Can children spot the pattern? (One-syllable words usually end in ck.)

6 Using suffixes to change word class

<table>
<tr><td colspan="2">Objective for Unit 6
To change nouns and adjectives into verbs by the use of suffixes</td></tr>
</table>

Part 1 | You need

Big Book page 12; dry-wipe boards or notebooks; Pupil's Book pages 12–13; PCM 6

Whole class
- Focus pupils on the BBk page. Explain that the word factory creates verbs by adding ate, en, ify or ise to different nouns and adjectives.
- Take each word from the basket in turn and turn it into a verb by adding a suffix. Children spell suggestions on dry-wipe boards.
- Discuss how spellings change, e.g. dropping the y or e at the end of a word.
- Write a short passage using the verbs made, e.g. *They watched the pool thicken and flatten like a board. The sky began to lighten and the shadows lengthened.*
- Introduce the oddbod: *change* – see below.

Pupil activities
A: Change nouns and adjectives into verbs.
B: Add ate, en, ify, ise suffixes.
C: Change nouns and adjectives into verbs.

Extra challenge: Make a verb from *liquid*.

Review
- Recap: you can change the use of a word (word class) by adding a suffix.
- Recap spelling rules. Most words just add the suffix. The y changes to i when adding ness. When a root word ends in e or y this is dropped. Some other words change their spelling more dramatically, e.g. *medicine – medicate* (drop ine).

Homework
Change adjectives and nouns into verbs by adding the suffixes ise, en, ify and ate.

Oddbod change
- On dry-wipe boards, jot down the letters that make the opening sound (ch).
- Link it to the rhyming word *strange*.
- Mnemonic – *chips are not greasy enough.*

Snip-snap Choose the Suffix
- Write up a choice of suffixes, e.g. tion, ity, ness.
- Say a word (e.g. *cool, stupid, attend, deaf, like, good, dark, celebrate, elect, pure*).
- Children write the noun on dry-wipe boards, using the correct suffix.

NLS objective for Unit 6

4.1.W14

Part 2 | You need   Big Book page 13; dry-wipe boards or notebooks

Whole class
- Quickly revisit the previous session. Discuss what happens to words that end in y or e. (y changes to i and the e is dropped)
- Focus on the BBk page. Explain that this word factory can change verbs back into nouns by adding tion.
- Take each verb and turn it into a noun by adding the suffix tion.
- Children spell the new words on dry-wipe boards.
- Look at the way the e gets dropped, e.g. *pollute – pollution* and note spelling changes, e.g. *add* + ition, *examine* + ation, *intend* + tion.
- Write some sentences together, e.g. *The invitation arrived too late for Cinderella. The giant was a welcome addition to the party. To learn how to fly you have to take an examination.*

Review
- Point out that 85% of words that end in **shun** are spelled tion.
- Do not use sh for a **shun** ending except for catch-you-outs *cushion* and *fashion*. Make up a mnemonic, e.g. *shhh, cushions are in fashion!*
- Recap spelling rules: when a root word ends in e, this letter is dropped (e.g. *create – creation*); just add ion to words ending in t (e.g. *subtract – subtraction*). Some words change spelling dramatically (e.g. *repeat – repetition*).

- Homework review.
- Discuss results, focusing on root words which change their spelling.

Follow-up homework
Make a note of the suffixes in your spelling log. Note some examples of spelling changes, e.g. *create – creation, apology – apologise.*

Test dictation
OB For a change we had cake and ice-cream for tea.
A   We had to memorise some words from the dictionary.
    Those boys always terrorise the other children.
B   Jan was sorry and wanted to apologise.
    Jeff had to purify the water before he sipped it.
C   In February I will give you an invitation to my birthday party.

Snip-snap   Key Word Basketball
- Divide the class into two teams.
- Choose a word from the medium frequency word list and ask one child to spell it (to shoot hoop), matching the word to the child's spelling ability. A correct spelling = a slam dunk (point scored).
- Give the next word to a child in the opposite team.
- An incorrect spelling is automatically passed to the other team.

Snip-snap   Verbs into Nouns
- Write *globe* on the board and establish what part of speech it is (noun).
- Ask the children to change it to a verb by adding ise (*globalise*).
- Take another example (e.g. *drama, hospital*) and explore it in the same way.

7 Adding suffixes

Objective for Unit 7

To spell the suffixes ship, hood, ness, ment

Part 1

You need Big Book page 14; dry-wipe boards or notebooks;
Pupil's Book pages 14–15; PCM 7

Whole class
- Explain that the suffixes – ship, hood, ness, ment – describe a state of being (e.g. *childhood – the state of being a child, contentment – being content*).
- Focus pupils on the BBk page. Read through the passage and ask children to complete the words in brackets on dry-wipe boards, adding the appropriate suffix, dom, ish, some, ment, ness, ship or hood.
- Get Up and Go: ask children with the correct spelling to write the word on the board.
- Note that *wise* changes to *wisdom*, dropping the e. Listen to the change in pronunciation to aid spelling.
- Look at the ment examples and discuss the change in word class (ment can change verbs to nouns, e.g. *enjoy – enjoyment*).
- Similarly, look at ness examples (ness can change adjectives to nouns, e.g. *cheerful – cheerfulness*). Point out that y changes to i in *happy – happiness*.
- Continue the story together, using the same suffixes, e.g. *We must avoid such carelessness and foolishness in future …*
- Introduce the oddbod: *being* – see below.

Pupil activities
A: Choose the right suffix, ment or ness, and note spelling changes.
B: Choose the right suffix, ment or ness, and complete a chart.
C: Write an ish poem.

Extra challenge: Work out the meaning of the suffix craft.

Review
- Recap that a number of suffixes help to describe states of being, e.g. ship, hood, ness and ment.
- Usually, you just add the suffix, but watch out for a final y that might change to i.

Homework
Add suffixes dom, like, ish, some, ment, ness and ship.

Oddbod being 📝
- Easy – take the word *be* and add on ing. (It has nothing to do with the stinging *bee*! That would give us *beeing* – does that look right?)
- Speed write *being*.

Snip-snap Word Building ✌
- Write up a suffix (e.g. hood). Say a root word (e.g. for hood: *child, false, boy, monk, false, knight, baby, likely, lively, neighbour, sister, father, mother, parent*).
- Children put thumbs up or down depending on whether a proper word can be made by joining the two.

<table>
<tr><td>

NLS objective for Unit 7

4.1.W9
</td></tr>
</table>

Part 2 | You need   Big Book page 15; dry-wipe boards or notebooks

Whole class
- Briefly revisit the previous session: adding suffixes to root words.
- Explain that you will now look at ness in more detail.
- Focus pupils on the Big Book page and point out that a useful way to remember how to spell the suffix is by thinking of Loch Ness.
- Read the rap together.
- Get Up and Go: children identify the ness words, underlining roots in one colour and suffixes in another.
- Discuss meanings of the words and their roots.
- Look at what happens to words ending in y, e.g. *ugly*, *shabby* (y changes to i), but compare with *grey* (vowel + y) where ness is simply added.
- Look at the second and third verses and the examples of multiple suffixes. Break down *helplessness*, *gracefulness* and *fearlessness* (e.g. *help* + less + ness = noun > adjective > noun).
- Write further verses with additional ness words, e.g. *hopelessness, foolishness, wariness, carelessness, noisiness, greediness, naughtiness*.

Review
- Recap that the suffix ness means 'being ...' (e.g. *carefulness* = being careful).
- It can be used to change adjectives into nouns (e.g. *kind – kindness*).
- Some words can take multiple suffixes (e.g. *childishness, carelessness*).

- Homework review.
- Ask children to share the words they have made, and put them into pairs.

Follow-up homework   Make a note of the suffixes in your spelling log, adding a few examples.

Test dictation
OB The children stopped being silly right away.
A   Fairness is very important in sport.
    Liz was told off for her silliness.
B   Sally found happiness with her new friends.
    Everyone should look after the environment.
C   My selfish brother doesn't know how to share.

Snip-snap Ron and Ern 🎧
- *Government* and *environment* are tricky words. It's easy to miss out the n.
- Use over-pronunciation to help – en-vi-<u>ron</u>-ment (*there's a* Ron *in* environ*ment*), gov-<u>ern</u>-ment (*there's an* Ern *in* gov*ern*ment).
- Learn these as a pair – 'Ron and Ern'.

Snip-snap Key Word Challenge ✍
- Use the key word list, focusing on 'regular' words that can be spelled easily.
- As you say a word, everyone writes it on dry-wipe boards. Then pairs check each other's spelling.
- Everyone starts with a score of ten. One point is lost per error.

Objective for Unit 8

To add suffixes to words ending in **f**

Part 1 | You need

Big Book page 16; dry-wipe boards or notebooks;
Pupil's Book pages 16–17; PCM 8

Whole class

- Focus pupils on the BBk page. Circle the rhyming words.
- Children write the singular forms on dry-wipe boards.
- Time Out: children sort the rhyming words into four columns, sorting by their spelling in the singular and thinking about what happens when they become plural.
- Ask the children to suggest the rules for making them plural.
  - words that end in ff (*snuffs, cuffs*) – add s
  - words that end in f (*leaves, thieves*) – drop f and add ves
  - words that end in ef (*handkerchiefs, beliefs*) – add s
  - words that end in fe (*knives, wives*) – add ves
- Compose some sentences together, trying to use the singular and plural form in the same sentence, e.g. *Put the knife with the other knives. My scarf is better than the other scarves.*
- Introduce the oddbod: *half*.

Pupil activities

A: Create plurals in spelling sums.
B: Change rhymes from singular to plural.
C: Change from plural to singular in a letter.

Extra challenge: Find catch-you-outs that can be spelt either way.

Review

- Recap: most words ending in **f** add s in the plural. Some words change to ves. Words ending in ff just add s. Words ending in fe change to ves.
- Sometimes a ves ending is used to change word class from noun to verb, e.g. *proof – proves, grief – grieves.*

Homework

Change sentences from singular to plural and vice versa.

Oddbod   half
- It rhymes with *calf*.
- Over-pronounce the l – 'hallllf'.
- Make up a mnemonic, e.g. *Alf got cut in half.*
- Speed write *half*: how many times in 30 seconds?

Snip-snap   Word Association
- As an individual or paired activity, think of as many words as possible linked to *half*, in two minutes.
- Share the findings: the person or pair with most associations correctly spelled wins.

<table>
<tr><td colspan="2">

NLS objective for Unit 8

4.2.W5
</td></tr>
</table>

Part 2 | You need   Big Book page 17; dry-wipe boards or notebooks

Whole class
- Quickly revisit the previous session: plurals of words ending in **f**.
- Focus on the BBk page. Read the poem.
- Show Me: children use the pictures to act as clues to guess the missing words. They write and show their spellings on dry-wipe boards.
- Discuss and refer to the rules found in the previous session – do they hold good?
- Note that in the penultimate couplet, *gloves* and *doves* are different, because the singular doesn't end in f. It just so happens that the plural shares the ves spelling pattern.
- Together, write a few couplets continuing the poem, e.g. *Each wife had seven cuffs, / Too many sniffs and too many snuffs. / Each wife had seven shelves, / One for the bloke and the rest for themselves.*

Review
- Recap: most words ending in **f** add s in the plural. Some words change to ves. Words ending in ff just add s. Words ending in fe change to ves.
- Homework review.
- Discuss children's results and work on some more sentences using plurals of words ending in **f**.

Follow-up homework
- Write an additional verse or verses for the St Ives poem.

Test dictation
- OB The invitation said that we should come at half past four.
- A   They say cats have nine lives.
         A cook needs to have lots of knives.
- B   My brothers both have new wives.
         The scary wolves terrorise everyone in the wood.
- C   I went shopping to get a better pair of gloves.

Snip-snap   Plural to Singular
- Write a plural on the board, e.g. *elves*.
- Children spell the singular on dry-wipe boards. Alternatively, you can write the singular form and children write the plural.
- Have reminder rules on display for children to refer to.

Snip-snap   Riddles Game
- Give a clue to a word ending in f, e.g. *The enemy of Little Red Riding Hood*.
- Children write the answer on dry-wipe boards, giving singular and plural, on board, e.g. *wolf – wolves*.
- Try using: *elf, half, leaf, loaf, scarf, thief, cliff, puff, knife, life, wife*.

9 Common word endings

<table>
<tr><td colspan="2">Objective for Unit 9
To spell words with common endings</td></tr>
</table>

Part 1 | You need

Big Book page 18; dry-wipe boards or notebooks;
Pupil's Book pages 18–19; PCM 9

Whole class
- Focus on the BBk page. Read the poem through, chanting together.
- Ask the class to identify the words that end in the **ight** sound.
- Who can spot the different ways to spell this sound? Which way is the most common?
- Ask children to list more words with the **ight** sound.
- Together, add further verses, e.g. *Two might like to fight, / But are too thin and slight. / Two ran from left to right, / Wearing trousers far too tight.*
- Introduce the oddbod: *might* – see below.

Pupil activities

A: Choose ight or ite spellings and devise an ight mnemonic.
B: Finish a story using ight or ite words.
C: Brainstorm ight and ough words.

Extra challenge: Find the root words in a passage.

Review
- Knowing common endings can be useful for spelling.
- Always listen for the common endings that may help you spell.

Homework

Find the origins of the days of the week.

Oddbod   might 👁 💭
- The spelling could be confused with *mite*, *meight* (as in *height*) or *myte*.
- Take a 'picture' – look at the word and hold it in your memory.
- Make up a mnemonic, e.g. *Many Insects Go Home Tonight*.

Snip-snap   Quick Rhyme
- Say the word *night*.
- Children use dry-wipe boards to list as many rhymes as possible in one minute.
- Score one point for each rhyming word that is spelt correctly.

NLS objective for Unit 9
4.2.W6

Part 2 | You need   Big Book page 19; dry-wipe boards or notebooks

Whole class
- Quickly revisit previous session: the suffix ight.
- Focus on the BBk page. Introduce the common word endings.
- Children work on dry-wipe boards in pairs, taking the word beginnings and adding the ending.
- Ask children to show their spellings. Discuss meanings.
- Add other words that have the same ending.
- Together, write a short passage using some of the words, e.g. *Although there is a lot, it's not enough. The question is about pollution.*

Review
- Recap: most words that end in the **ight** sound are spelt ight – the most common exceptions are *white* and *kite*. Most words that end in a **shun** sound are spelled tion (though some are spelled sion – see Unit 17). This is usually easy to hear from the pronunciation, as is ious as an ending. The ial ending usually is preceded by c, e.g. *racial*. The ending ough is harder to pin down. Common words such as *through, although, though, enough, rough* just have to be learned.

- Homework review.
- Ask children to share their answers, making sure that they can see the link between the word and its root.

Follow-up homework
List the common endings in your spelling log and note a few examples.
Also write down the most common ough spellings.

Test dictation
OB "I might come too after I have rested for a while," said Dad.
A   You will look silly if your trousers are too tight.
     The pop star was caught in the spotlight.
B   The little brown rabbit took a bite of the carrot.
     Pete could fly a kite very well.
C   The wind blew harder and the sea got very rough.

Snip-snap   Got Enough?
- Speed write the suffix ough – how many times in 30 seconds?
- Say an ough word – children spell it on dry-wipe boards. Try: *cough, tough, enough, rough, dough, plough, although, through.*

Snip-snap   Reveal
- Select a word and write up the first letter.
- Children guess what the word might be and spell it on dry-wipe boards.
- Write up the second letter.
- Continue, letter by letter, until someone guesses and correctly spells the word.

10 Prefixes <u>al</u>, <u>ad</u> and <u>af</u>

Objective for Unit 10	
To recognise and spell prefixes al, ad and af	

Part 1 | **You need** | Big Book page 20; dry-wipe boards or notebooks; coloured pens; Pupil's Book pages 20–21; PCM 10

Whole class
- Revisit the definition of a prefix: letters or words that are added to a word to change its meaning.
- Focus on the BBk page. Read the instruction.
- Discuss what will happen to all when it is added to the base word (it drops one l). So a word beginning with al means 'all' plus the base word or root.
- Invite children to make the new words with the al prefix by having a go on dry-wipe boards or by writing on the book.
- When children offer words beginning with a plus a base word or root beginning with l, e.g. *aloft, alone, alert*, etc., treat these as catch-you-outs. They do not have the al prefix, but the a prefix. Demonstrate how al is pronounced 'all', whereas the catch-you-outs are not.
- Write some sentences together using some of the words you have made or any others that the class can think of, e.g. *We almost always allow Alison and the others to sing alto altogether.*
- Introduce the oddbod: *any*.

Pupil activities
A: Add the prefix al to the root.
B: Complete the cloze using al words.
C: Complete the spelling of al words from clues.

Think about ...: Looking for prefixes or suffixes when spelling a word.

Review
- Recap: al means 'all' and drops one of the ls but still says 'all'. Review the exceptions.

Homework
Write some class rules using as many words with al prefixes as possible.

Oddbod   any
- Break the word into two syllables – a-ny. It says 'tum-ti' – the a is stressed but actually sounds like e.
- There is no prefix: this is just a word that happens to begin with a.
- Think of compound words using *any*.
- Can the children tell you how to spell *many*?

Snip-snap   All Change!
- Take an al word (e.g. *always, already, although, altogether, also, almost*).
- Change the pronunciation, e.g. *al – ways*.
- Practise spelling as a group – emphasising that all becomes al.
- Make up a mnemonic, e.g. *All becomes American 'Al'* (as in Al Pacino).

28

NLS objective for Unit 10
4.2.W7

Part 2 | You need   Big Book page 21; dry-wipe boards or notebooks

Whole class

■ Quickly revisit the previous session: adding al prefixes.

■ Revisit the idea of a prefix generally being unstressed (*apply* has a 'ti-tum' rhythm as opposed to *apple* which has a 'tum-ti' rhythm). It is particularly important to note this whilst focusing on prefixes beginning with a because of the need to distinguish between those which are prefixes and those which are simply words beginning with a.

■ Focus on the BBk page. Read the prefixes ad and af and discuss their meaning. Both mean 'towards'.

■ Read the base words and decide which prefix each one should fly to. Invite children to draw the flight path to the target.

■ Discuss the rule for adding ad and af (just add ad, but add af when the word begins with f to make a double ff).

■ Try adding further words to the ad and af collection. (Note *after, afar* and *afraid* as exceptions.)

Review

■ Recap the helpful rules that for ad just add it; af, rather than ad, is added to words beginning with f; al has dropped one l from all.

■ Recap the meanings of the prefixes and point out that af and ad mean the same (towards) but the letters change to make the pronunciation easier.

■ Homework review.

■ Ask the children to share some of their rules and write them up on a class poster.

Follow-up homework

Make a note in your spelling log of the main al, ad, af words that you need to use and find difficult. Jot down a way to remember that when adding all you drop one l, e.g. *altogether*.

Test dictation

OB We haven't got any additions this week.
A   The thief worked alone in the night.
     Sue also has a bad cough.
B   Those boys have got into a fight already.
     The bright light keeps me awake.
C   My puppy is foolish but full of adventure.

Snip-snap   Words Within a Word
■ Write up *altogether* on the board.
■ Children look for words within the word and write down as many as they can within two minutes.

Snip-snap   Plus Word Endings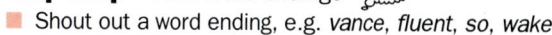
■ Shout out a word ending, e.g. *vance, fluent, so, wake*.
■ Children write a suitable prefix on dry-wipe boards, e.g. ad, af, al or a.

11 Prefix roundup

Objectives for Unit 11

To recognise and spell common prefixes

Part 1

You need   Big Book page 22, dry-wipe boards or notebooks;
Pupil's Book pages 22–23; PCM 11

Whole class
- Recap the meaning of *prefix*: a bit you add to the beginning of a root word to change its meaning; pre means 'in front of'.
- Remind children that prefixes are easy – you don't have to change the spelling of the root word, you just add them.
- Recap on Y3 term 1 work (Unit 4), adding negative prefixes to make antonyms, e.g. *happy – unhappy*.
- Look at the BBk page. Cover up the middle column headed 'meaning'.
- Look through the list together, asking children to contribute words for some of the prefixes.
- Try and work out the meaning of some of the prefixes. Then reveal the middle column.
- Ask volunteers to give the meaning of individual words, e.g. *foretell* – 'tell beforehand'.
- Work out other meanings together, showing the children how to use the dictionary and read any notes on derivations which will give clues to meaning.
- Look at *de-ice*. Can the children guess why it has a hyphen? How would you pronounce the word if it didn't have a hyphen? Find other examples, e.g. *co-operate*. Work out the rule – a hyphen separates two vowels.
- Introduce the oddbod: *until* – see below.

Pupil activities
A: Add the prefix un.
B: Add the prefix over and give meanings.
C: Think of words for a given prefix and work out meanings.

Extra challenge: Make a list of common English prefixes.

Review
- Knowing which is the root word and which bit is the prefix can help you to spell words and remember word families.
- Ask the children to contribute some of the words they have made.
- Count up how many different prefixes you have collected altogether and discuss meanings.

Homework   Make a prefix word wheel.

Oddbod   until
- The tricky bit is to remember that it only has one l; otherwise it is phonically regular.
- Make up an acronym: *Unicorns never talk in lessons*.
- Clap out the rhythm as you say each letter.

Snip-snap   Dictionary Chase
- Write words on the board which can take a negative prefix, e.g. *happy, take, appear, interested, read, honest, believe, behave, solve, fortune, lead, trust, qualify, possible, legible*.
- Working in pairs, children race to add a negative prefix to each word and check its meaning in the dictionary.

NLS objectives for Unit 11

4.2.W7   4.2.W8

Part 2 | **You need**   Big Book page 23; dry-wipe boards or notebooks

Whole class
- Focus on the BBk page. Read the wizard's potion aloud together.
- Time Out: in pairs children add prefixes to the gaps to make words.
- Get Up and Go: volunteers provide the words.
- Together, write a final couple of sentences to complete the potion, if possible incorporating a prefix or two, e.g. *She will be transformed immediately into an unusually ungainly frog.*
- Be prepared to give a dramatic rendering of teacher turning into frog when the potion is complete!

Review
- Homework review.
- Ask the children to contribute their homework words and add them to the class prefix collection.
- Remind them that prefixes are easy – you just add them to the front of the root word.
- Emphasise that even when the prefix ends with the same letter as the first letter in the root word, it's still easy! You just have a double letter.
- Suggest that the children could make up meanings for some of the new 'words' they made that don't exist yet!

Follow-up homework
Children write their own potion using prefixes or find a recipe and identify the prefixes.

Test dictation
OB   "I will keep walking until I get home," said Fran.
A   You should unplug the light before you go to bed.
     I'm sorry that my room is always so untidy.
B   The bath was too full and started to overflow.
     Dan's racing car is going to overtake Sue's.
C   In hospital they prescribe pills to help you get better.

Snip-snap   Prefix Pelmanism
- Ask the children to write out prefixes and roots on separate cards.
- Working in pairs, they spread their cards out face down.
- Each child turns up two cards. If the cards make a word, keep the pair and win a point. If they don't, turn them face down again and continue.
- The player with the most pairs is the winner.

Snip-snap   Key Word Sort
- Give pairs of children about 20 words each from the key word list.
- Ask them to sort the words into sets in any way they choose, e.g. number of letters, vowel sounds, consonant clusters, parts of speech, words with the same initial or final letter, number of syllables.
- Pairs then present two examples of their sets.
- Others try and guess what the criteria were.

12 Letter strings w + vowel, ss

Objective for Unit 12

To explore the occurrence of letter strings

Part 1 | **You need** Big Book page 24; dry-wipe boards or notebooks; dictionaries; Pupil's Book pages 24–25; PCM 12

Whole class
- Focus on the BBk page, covering up the chart. Read the sentence together.
- Ask the children to identify what the words have in common.
- Get Up and Go: ask individuals to ring the wa letter strings.
- Ask the children where the letter strings occur. Fill in the chart on the page.
- Sum up your findings: wa generally comes at the beginning of a word or often after s; sometimes in the middle (e.g. *towards*).
- Elicit or point out that swa is a common letter string. Ask children to brainstorm other swa words, writing them on dry-wipe boards, e.g. *swap, swam, swagger, swag, swarm, sway.*
- Compose a swa tongue twister together, e.g. *swallow a swarm of swaggering swashbucklers.*
- Consider the letter strings wo, wi: speculate whether the same is true for these but leave it for the children to investigate in independent work.
- Introduce the oddbod: *guess* – see below.

Pupil activities
A: Find words with letter strings wa and wo.
B: Find words with letter strings wi, wa and wo, and use them in a short story.
C: Investigate letter strings wi, wu.

Extra challenge: Find out if wo or wa can come at the end of a word.

Review
- Ask children from different groups to contribute findings from their letter string investigations.
- Remind them of the catch-you-outs, e.g. *what* and *which*, which sound as if they belong to the wo and wi set but don't.
- *Sword* is worth noting, where the w is silent.
- *Swum* and *swung* are rare swu words.
- *Two* is the only example of a wo ending – there are no wa endings in English.
- Point out how many different sounds wa and wo can make, e.g. i as in *women*, oo as in *wound*.

Homework Make up a wo and wa tongue twister.

Oddbod guess
- Link it to other hissing words (see Part 2).
- Link it to previous work on silent letters.
- Invent a mnemonic, e.g. *guess where the u is.*

Snip-snap Letter String Link
- Start the children off with a common letter string, e.g. spa.
- Keeping up a quick pace, each child or pair contributes a word beginning with that string, writing it on the board or holding up dry-wipe boards.
- When ideas run out, change the letter string, e.g. cha.

<table>
<tr><td colspan="3">**NLS objectives for Unit 12**</td></tr>
<tr><td>4.2.W4</td><td>4.2.W8</td><td>4.3.W5</td></tr>
</table>

Part 2 | **You need** — Big Book page 25; dry-wipe boards or notebooks

Whole class

- Focus on the BBk page and read the instruction.
- Do the children know the meaning of *missive*? (a letter)
- Then read the beginning of the letter and discuss why it's 'hissing'.
- Read the surrounding words and use them, and any others generated by the children, to expand the hissing missive, e.g. *I was cross and helpless. My boss guessed I was stressed and asked me to discuss it. If possible please send me a message. Bless you. Yours passionately Ross Prosser.*
- Time Out: pairs can think of their own ideas using their dry-wipe boards.
- Incidentally, point out the exception *bus*. You might tell the children its origin – an abbreviation of the Latin word *omnibus* (*omni* = 'for all').

Review

- Emphasise that it's useful to investigate common letter strings because it helps you to work out likely spellings.
- ss is most common at the ends of words because of suffixes less and ness. Note how it changes to the **sh** sound when you add ion, e.g. *percussion*.
- Listen to some of the oddbod stories, commenting on differences and similarities: if time, work on one perfect class version.
- Homework review.
- Ask children to share some of their tongue twisters and get volunteers to say them as fast as they can.

Follow-up homework

Investigate which consonants can follow s in a word, e.g. sc, sh, sk, sl, and collect examples of each combination.

Test dictation

OB Can you guess what colour my new kite is?
A   If something is too warm it can overheat.
    Pam had a bad leg and was unable to walk.
B   The children were walking towards the library.
    You must beware of the wolves in the dark wood.
C   A swift and a swallow are both birds.

Snip-snap   Hiss and Miss

- Call out a word at a time from the following list: *bus, does, this, has, guess, was, his, hiss, goes, across, success, pass, goodness, faces, discussion, fuss, always, lesson.*
- Children stand up if they think the word has a double s in it – score a point if correct.
- Show Me: spell on the board for another point.

Snip-snap   Key Word Sentence Race

- Use the NLS list for Year 4 term 2. Give pairs of children four key words each – they write them down.
- Pairs race to make a sentence with all their words.
- The winning pair says their sentence and spells the key words.

13 Investigating k, v and l

Objective for Unit 13

To explore the occurrence of certain letters

Part 1

You need Big Book page 26; dry-wipe boards or notebooks; Pupil's Book pages 26–27; PCM 13

Whole class

- Explain that it is useful to investigate the letter k because it has some habits which can help you to remember spellings.
- Brainstorm some words which start with k and scribe them on the board.
- Ask the children to write other words ending in ck on their dry-wipe boards.
- Does k ever come in the middle of words as well as at the beginning and end? Ask volunteers to suggest words, e.g. *take*, *tickle*, and scribe on the board.
- Then look at the BBk page. How many words have the children already thought of? Tick them off on the page.
- Have the children thought of any that aren't in the BBk?
- Brainstorm rhyming words for common endings, e.g. *back*, *crack*, *shack*.
- Start a simple rhyme, e.g. *Uncle Jack / Lived in a shack*, and ask the children to provide more lines, e.g. *Went to Wales and never came back / Fell down a hole and broke his back.*
- Introduce the oddbod: *across* – see below.

Pupil activities

A: Find rhyming k words.
B: Sort k words and find some rhymes.
C: Sort the k words in a poem, then add to the poem.

Extra challenge: Find words ending with a vowel and k.

Review

- Listen to C group's pack of tricks poems.
- Summarise: k often goes with c at the end of words, especially with 'short' vowels. Other common combinations are nk, lk, rk. In the middle of words, k usually follows a 'long' vowel, ck a 'short' vowel (e.g. *crackle*, *take*). Compare with *ankle* (k follows a consonant).
- *Kayak*, *wok* and *yak* are examples of catch-you-outs with no c. All are foreign imports.

Homework

Investigate l letter strings.

Oddbod across 💭
- Link it to other ss endings (see Unit 12).
- Group with *along*: both are a prepositions describing direction (see Unit 10).

Snip-snap Letter Hunt 👁
- Give the children dictionaries between pairs.
- Allocate different letters for pairs to investigate (c, p, g, h, q, t, x, y).
- Pairs find examples of each letter at the beginning, middle and end of words.
- Investigate particularly common combinations, e.g. ch, th, sh, wh, ing, ex.
- Compile lists for classroom display.

NLS objectives for Unit 13

4.3.W3   4.3.W4   4.3.W5

Part 2 | You need   Big Book page 27; dry-wipe boards or notebooks

Whole class
- Focus on the BBk page. Give the children time to recognise the advertisement genre and the recurring letter v.
- Discuss what they have noticed.
- Ask individuals to ring examples of the letter v.
- Are there any patterns emerging? (e.g. *vita* beginning)
- Can other consonants go with v? (e.g. *swerve, solve, invent*) Mostly, however, v is next to a vowel.
- Together, write some rules about using v in the 'Have a go' box.
- Write a slogan using words from the BBk list – either as a shared activity or in pairs on dry-wipe boards, e.g. *Vote for Victor's favourite variety!*

Review
- Ask children to recap what they know about the letter v (usually occurs next to a vowel at the beginning or middle of words).
- Can they think of an example with double v in the middle of a word (e.g. *revving*) or at the end of a word (no examples)? What about as a single letter at the end of a word? (no, it's always followed by e, e.g. *have, same*)
- Collect children's names spelt with k or v, e.g. *Vanesh, Valerie, Kenneth, Keith.*

- Homework review.
- Children think about which other consonants can follow l at the end of a word.

Follow-up homework
- Children write out their own advert using any of the v words from the whole-class session.

Test dictation
- OB Pat's sister went through the door and across the room.
- A   Cold weather can make you cough.
       I will take my brother to play on the swing.
- B   The wizard did another good trick.
       Dad's clock had stopped working.
- C   Jim's mum gave me some milk and a cracker.

Snip-snap   Fish and Chips 👁 💬
- Allocate pairs to two teams – 'Fish' and 'Chips'.
- Pairs list as many words as they can find with examples of their team's letter string (ch or sh).
- Write up each team's words.
- Sh doesn't often come in the middle of words (exceptions *cushion, fashion*). Here, the **sh** sound is generally spelt ti or si, especially if followed by on, e.g. *action, passion.*

Snip-snap   a and b Key Words ✍
- Children work in pairs, with one child as 'a' and the other 'b'.
- Using the NLS list for Year 4, pairs test each other on any words beginning with a and b.
- Race to spell as many as possible on dry-wipe boards before the egg timer runs out.
- Add up points (one point for every individual correct spelling).

Same spelling, different pronunciation

Objective for Unit 14

To spell words with common letter strings but different pronunciations

---

Part 1 | **You need** | Big Book page 28; dry-wipe boards or notebooks; Pupil's Book pages 28–29; PCM 14

Whole class
- Focus on the BBk page and read the poem aloud together.
- What is it about? Why does English pronunciation make you dizzy? Prompt the children to understand that the same letter strings often have different pronunciations.
- Get Up and Go: ask volunteers to highlight pairs or groups of letter strings in words which are pronounced differently, e.g. ea, or, ear, ew, ie.
- What does the title mean? And what is odd about the word *chaos*? Compare it with other cha words, e.g. *chair*, *charge*.
- Look at the word *tear* in line 7. Recap the term *homograph* – a word that looks the same as another but doesn't sound or mean the same.
- Write letter string headings on the board: ou, ice, ear.
- Time Out: in pairs, children write examples of words with different pronunciations for each heading: e.g. *police*, *nice*, *notice*.
- Which pronunciation is the most/least common? Are there any patterns? Look for rhyming sets.
- Introduce the letter string ough with the oddbod *though* – see below.

Pupil activities
A: Find the odd one out – ow letter string sounds.
B: Find ou letter string words with different sounds.
C: Sort ough letter string words.

Extra challenge: Find words ending in eight.

Review
- Ask groups to contribute words to a class collection – discuss how to display this.
- Emphasise that collecting sets of words with the same letter strings helps with spelling.

Homework
Investigate gh.

Oddbod though
- Link this with other ough words (*thought*, *cough*, etc.).
- Find the word within the word: *thou*.
- Make up mnemonics, e.g. *though thou and I must part*.

Snip-snap i before e except after c Investigation
- Some of the children may already know this spelling 'rule': is it true?
- Test it out by collecting examples of ie letter strings, e.g. *chief, thief, piece, field, dies, diet* (look at pronunciation differences).
- Find examples of ei after c, e.g. *receive, ceiling*.
- Prompt exceptions if necessary, e.g. *science, height, weight* (note pronunciation).
- Look at names which break the 'rule', e.g. *Sheila, Keith, Neil*.

NLS objective for Unit 14
4.3.W6

Part 2 | **You need**   Big Book page 29; dry-wipe boards or notebooks

Whole class

- Homework review.
- Discuss findings from the gh homework investigation.

- Point out that it's mainly the vowel strings that vary in sound, although some consonant strings have more than one pronunciation, e.g. ch, gh.
- Look at how it changes the preceding vowel sound. It helps to remember the words in sets.

- Focus on the BBk page. Look at the picture together and ask individual children to read the speech bubbles.
- Establish that each bubble contains a non-rhyme.
- Get Up and Go: ask volunteers to circle the letter strings which are the same but which do not rhyme.
- Compose some more bubbles using common strings, e.g. *limb*, *climb*; *shoes*, *goes*; *rough*, *cough*.
- Encourage the children to refer to words in their collections or from the poem on BBk page 28.

Review

- Explain that there are more sounds (over 40) than there are letters (26) in our language, so the same letters have to be used for more than one sound.
- Emphasise that's not as difficult as it seems! Most words belong to a set, so look for patterns and collect word families.

Follow-up homework

- Investigate words where the letter string ou is pronounced in different ways (e.g. *rough*, *through* and *mould*).

Test dictation

- OB   Though it was cold, the sun was very bright.
- A   The ball went right through the broken window.
  Please could you show me where the hospital is?
- B   I would like to apologise for my clumsiness.
  Sam's journey began as soon as it was light.
- C   "Do you think I have bought enough cake?" asked Mum.

Snip-snap   String-along Tens (or fives)

- Write the chosen letter string on the board, or on individual dry-wipe boards, e.g. ice, au, ie, ight.
- Within a time limit, pairs race to find ten words with at least two different sounds.
- Score an extra point for any word nobody else has got.

Snip-snap   Quick-fire Quiz

- Use the Year 4 NLS list and give the children a series of problems. Ask them to write, e.g.:
  – a word with two a's (or three/four a's);
  – words with a double consonant in them;
  – words with double vowels;
  – a word with three consonants in a row;
  – a word with three different vowels.

15 Common roots

Objective for Unit 15

To collect and classify words with common roots

Part 1 | **You need** Big Book page 30; dry-wipe boards or notebooks; Pupil's Book pages 30–31; PCM 15

Whole class
- Recap the term *root* and explain its meaning – a word or part of a word, often from another language, to which you can join different prefixes and suffixes to make new words, e.g. *annual – anniversary* (from the Latin *annus* meaning 'year'), *clear – unclear – clearing*.
- Focus on the BBk page. Ask the children what they notice (e.g. each root can take both prefixes and suffixes).
- Discuss the meaning of the words.
- Can the children identify the root each time? Ask volunteers to circle the roots and the prefixes/suffixes in different colours.
- Can they guess the meanings of the roots? (L. *dictare/dicere* – to say; Fr. *presser* (from L. *pressare*) to press; Gr. *phone* – sound; L. *portare* – to carry)
- Explain that roots come from Latin and Greek.
- Explain that knowing common roots can help with spelling, especially with words that can be broken down, or words where the root has changed its sound, as in the case of *pressure*, where knowing the root can avoid confusing the **sh** sound.
- Choose one collection of words and compose a sentence, e.g. *The dictator predicted the verdict. I repressed the impression that he was under pressure.*
- Introduce the oddbod: *sure* – see below.

Pupil activities
A: Spot words with a common root and find others to add to the set.
B: Write sentences for words with common roots.
C: Write sentences for words with common roots.

Extra challenge: Use prefixes, suffixes and common roots to invent new words.

Review
- Knowing roots and prefixes and suffixes can help you build new words.
- Knowing roots can help you spell words you've never written before.
- English is made up of words from many different languages and many roots come from Latin and Greek.

Homework Think of two words from each of the Latin roots *aqua*, *annus*, *decem*, *unus*.

Oddbod sure
- Link it with words which include *sure* as the root, e.g. *unsure, surely, insure, assure.*
- Point out that *sure* and *sugar* are the only words where s is pronounced like sh.
- Collect compounds and phrases, e.g. *surefooted, for sure, sure enough, sure-fire.* Practise writing them out with handwriting joins.

Snip-snap Number Roots
- Write some number roots on the board, e.g. uni, bi, tri, quart.
- Establish what these roots mean.
- In pairs, children brainstorm derivations, e.g. *universe, unison, bicycle, binocular, triangle, tricycle, quartet, quarter.*
- Challenge them to find words with roots meaning 'eight' and 'ten' (e.g. *octopus, decade*).

Part 2 | **You need** Big Book page 31; dry-wipe boards or notebooks

Whole class

- Focus on the BBk page. Explain how a word web is built up – you start with one word and then branch off in different directions. Each list you make will give you new words to start new lists. Word webs can go on forever, or until there's no room left on the page.
- Trace the web from *telephone*: encourage the children to find other words to add and new lists to make, e.g. *mobile, mobilisation, mobility, mob*.
- Work out root meanings together.
- Then start creating your own word web around a suitable word (e.g. *transport*), using both parts of the word and making new links (e.g. *transmit* → *submit* → *submarine* → *mariner*).
- Use different colours to emphasise roots.

Review

- Recap some of the most common roots.
- Discuss how you might display collections in the classroom – as webs or word trees.

- Homework review.
- Look at homework discoveries and add more words to the collections.

Follow-up homework

Create original word webs starting with *transform* or *depart*.

Test dictation

OB Ned was sure he would be the winner of the competition.
A An octopus lives in the sea and has eight legs.
   The journey takes an hour by express bus.
B Mr Brown uses a tractor to plough his land.
   Pat read an extract from the book's introduction.
C The show we went to see last week was spectacular.

Snip-snap Pressure Point

- Start off with *press*. In pairs children add prefixes or suffixes to make new words on dry-wipe boards, using dictionaries to help.
- When they run out of ideas, set them off again with another root, e.g. *vent, form, scribe, fact*.
- Encourage them to beat their best record.

Snip-snap Beetle

- The same as Hangman but less gruesome!
- Think of a key word and write down a dash for each letter in the word.
- The children take it in turns to suggest one letter at a time.
- If the letter isn't in the word, draw a part of the beetle (three body parts, two feelers, six legs – generously allowing for eleven guesses per word).
- The game is useful for teaching probable letter sequences.

16 Suffix roundup

Objective for Unit 16
To practise extending and compounding words through adding parts

Part 1 | **You need** Big Book page 32; dry-wipe boards or notebooks; Pupil's Book pages 32–33; PCM 16

Whole class
- Recap the term *suffix*.
- Focus on the BBk page and study the first two columns together.
- Check the meaning of the suffixes ful (full of) and ly (in this way).
- Elicit or point out that often, the ly suffix turns an adjective into an adverb.
- Elicit that adding ful can turn a noun into an adjective.
- Look at *beautiful* and *merciful*. Do they remember the rule? (y changes to i when adding a consonant suffix)
- Focus on the ic suffix. Help the children to see that nouns ending in y (e.g. *energy*, *allergy*) drop the y before adding the suffix.
- Point out oddities: *comedy* drops edy to make *comic*. Sometimes the suffix has an extra bit, e.g. tific in *scientific*, etic in *energetic*.
- Look at the last column together. Point out that ive can turn both nouns and verbs into adjectives. Ask the children to identify the root words. What happens to words that end in e? (*expense*) Look at *explosive* and *decisive* – what has happened to the root? (de changes to s)
- Introduce the oddbod: *different* – see below.

Pupil activities
A: Make adverbs using ly.
B: Make adjectives using ive, ful.
C: Make nouns using ure, ment.

Extra challenge: Make adjectives from verbs using able.

Review
- Recap that ly and ful are consonant suffixes; most base words stay the same; words ending in y change to i (but note *play – playful*!).
- Two catch-you-outs are *wholly* and *awful*: ask the children to work out what happens in these cases.
- Suffixes ic, ist and ive drop the final e or y from the base word.
- Emphasise that ly can create adverbs, ful, ic and ive create adjectives.

Homework
Investigate ic.

Oddbod different
- Link it to the Snip-snap activity (see right).
- Identify the root word *differ*.
- Isolate the word within a word *rent*, and work out a mnemonic, e.g. *rent a different tent*.

Snip-snap Add-on Ants
- Write some ant and ent words on the board, e.g. *assistant, servant, president, independent, different, expectant, arrogant, pendant, repentant*.
- Work out the meanings, e.g. the first three are nouns meaning 'someone who…' (e.g. *assistant* means 'someone who assists').
- Point out the variation ant/ent and explain that there are no helpful rules – words just have to be learnt (see homework extra challenge).
- Brainstorm mnemonics, e.g. *ants aren't independent*; *presidents preside over America*.

40

NLS objective for Unit 16
4.3.W8

Part 2 | **You need**   Big Book page 33; dry-wipe boards or notebooks

Whole class
- Explain that there are over 300 suffixes in the English language.
- Focus on the BBk page, covering up all but the first column.
- Explain that the list shows some common suffixes.
- Time Out: in pairs, children think of examples and write them on dry-wipe boards.
- Reveal the last column, still keeping the middle column covered, and compare with the words the children have suggested.
- Note spelling points, e.g. y changes to i in *beautiful*, *happiness*; compare *baker* (loses the e) with *hopeless* (keeps the e).
- Relate ance, ence to ant, ent (see Snip-snap Add-on Ants in Part 1).
- Brainstorm base words which can have more than one suffix, e.g. *hopelessness*.
- Try to work out suffix meanings, then reveal the middle column and check.
- Make up a suffix-stuffed sentence (see Snip-snap below), e.g. *The beautiful actress had a hopeless childhood with no enjoyment or happiness until she married an engineer!* This could be shared or paired work.

Review
- Ask the children to give suffixes which make adverbs, adjectives or nouns.
- Recap rules: dropping or keeping e; changing y to i; dropping one l from *full*, etc.
- Homework review.
- Discuss children's results and highlight spelling patterns.

Follow-up homework
Practise **Look Say Cover Write Check** for new words with suffixes.

Test dictation
- OB My new book describes lots of different animals.
- A   The baby drank the warm milk sleepily.
       John made a suggestion helpfully.
- B   The school play this year was wonderful.
       The twins lived in an attractive house.
- C   Shopping is fun and gives me a lot of pleasure.

Snip-snap   Suffix-stuffed Sentences
- Write a cluster of suffixes on the board, e.g. less, ful, ly, ment, ive.
- In pairs, children race to produce a suffix-stuffed sentence using all the suffixes.
- Award extra points for any words with multiple suffixes, e.g. *thankfully*.

Snip-snap   Word Shapes
- Display about 10 key words with different lengths and outline shapes, e.g. *above, any, during, suddenly, half, morning, through, together, right, such*.
- Let pairs study the list, then conceal it.
- Draw an outline shape of one of the words, adding divisions to indicate the number of letters.
- In pairs, children write the word on dry-wipe boards.
- Fill in the shape on the board, drawing attention to particular features, e.g. ascenders or descenders.

17 Suffixes <u>ible</u>, <u>able</u> and <u>ion</u>

Objective for Unit 17

To recognise and spell the suffixes ible and able, tion and sion

---

Part 1 | **You need** | Big Book page 34; dry-wipe boards or notebooks; dictionaries; Pupil's Book pages 34–35; PCM 17

Whole class
- Remind the children of previous work on suffixes (see Unit 16).
- Introduce the two tricky variations: ible/able and tion/sion – many adults get these muddled up.
- Focus on the BBk page and study the first two columns.
- Ask the children to ring the root words and explain meanings.
- One clue to whether it's able or ible can be found looking at the root. If it's a recognisable verb then it's often able, e.g. *enjoyable*. You can add able to almost any verb to make a new word. Try a few, e.g. *work – workable*. But this doesn't always hold good – look for exceptions such as *reverse – reversible*.
- What happens if the root word ends in e? (e.g. *adore*) Ask the children to recall similar rules for adding other vowel suffixes, e.g. *explosive*, *machinist*.
- Look at the tion and sion lists, again identifying roots. Brainstorm more words to add to the two columns. Can children see any patterns? (e.g. sion often follows a verb that ends in de or se; the tion ending is often ation)
- Ask children to make new words by adding one of the suffixes to the root words below the chart.
- Model the use of a dictionary for checking spellings.
- Introduce the oddbod: *suddenly* – see below.

Pupil activities
A: Sort words ending in ible or able.
B: Add ible or able to roots to make new words.
C: Add ion to verbs to make nouns.

Think about ...: Check the spelling by seeing which ending looks right.

Review
- Ask the children to share new words from independent activities.
- Sum up: tion is more common than sion and is often preceded by an a. A verb that ends in de or se often takes sion.
- A general rule for ible and able is that verbs often take able.

Homework
Test grown-ups on words ending in ible/able, ion (tion, sion).

Oddbod   suddenly
- Identify the common suffix ly.
- Look for words within the word: *sud*, *den*, and use as a mnemonic to establish the double d.
- Practise the handwriting joins.

Snip-snap   Show Me   👁 👂
- Make two suffix cards for each child (or children could make them), ible and able on one side; tion and sion on the other.
- Say a word (e.g. *terrible*, *responsible*, *adorable*, *enjoyable*, *education*, *dictation*, *explosion*, *confusion*).
- Children hold up a suffix card showing the correct spelling.
- Keep up a brisk pace.
- If it's a happily competitive class, lives could be lost or handicaps given for each mistake.

NLS objectives for Unit 17

4.3.W3   4.3.W4   4.3.W9

Part 2 | You need   Big Book page 35; dry-wipe boards or notebooks

Whole class
- Focus on the BBk page and read the passage aloud together.
- Ask the children to identify all the ible and able words and to make two lists.
- Discuss meanings, particularly of more unfamilar words such as *inedible* and *vulnerable*.
- Revise the previous session by looking at the able list and identifying any root words (e.g. *adorable – adore*) and use these examples to reinforce rules of dropping a final e and changing y to i when adding a vowel suffix.
- Weave a story around the letter before carrying on with it. Use as many tion and sion words as possible while still keeping some sort of plot going (make use of the list on the BBk page). (e.g. *I am filled with confusion and emotion. If only we had not fallen for temptation. I fear the conclusion will be our execution. In expectation that this is my final communication.*)

Review
- Recap spelling patterns and rules for ible/able and ion (tion, sion).
- Reinforce by asking the children to provide examples.

- Homework review.
- Discuss homework findings.

Follow-up homework
- Rewrite the letter from the BBk, exchanging the ible, able, ion (sion, tion) words to change the meaning. The letter can be changed in places if necessary. NB: children will need to copy the letter out or you could make copies for them.

Test dictation
OB Suddenly Tom turned around and ran away quickly.
A   Mum bought me a dress that was suitable for school.
    I feel sad and miserable today.
B   Mum's attractive ring is very valuable.
    The wonderful book that I want is almost affordable.
C   The horrible traffic jam brought a lot of confusion.

Snip-snap   Wipe-out ⊙ ✍
- On the board, write a selection of about 10 ible/able and sion/tion words from the BBk.
- Give the children a few minutes to study the words.
- Hover dramatically over the board, so that the children don't know which word you're heading for, then swoop and wipe out one word.
- Say the word: children spell it on dry-wipe boards.
- Carry on until all the words have been wiped out, leaving the most tricky until last.

Snip-snap   Key Word Soccer ✍
- Two or more teams compete to spell key words from the NLS list for Y4 term 3 – or words frequently mis-spelt by your class.
- Each correct spelling scores a goal.
- Differentiate words according to individual players.

18 Diminutives

Objective for Unit 18

To form diminutives (by adding suffixes and prefixes)

| **Part 1** | **You need** | Big Book page 36; dry-wipe boards or notebooks; dictionaries and thesauruses; Pupil's Book pages 36–37; PCM 18 |

Whole class
- Remind the children that prefixes and suffixes can change the meaning of a word, e.g. *happy – unhappy, harmful – harmless*.
- Tell them that some prefixes and suffixes can change the size of something.
- Write the words *cab, book, duck* on the board.
- Give the children a moment or two to think of different add-ons to make them little, e.g. *minicab, booklet, duckling*.
- Highlight the prefixes and suffixes, then spend a few minutes using them to invent new words, e.g. *crisplet, miniburger, bunling*.
- Set new challenges, e.g. what could you call a young alien? (an *alienette*)
- Focus on the BBk page; explain small ads and tell children that all the things advertised are small.
- Time Out: children work in pairs, identifying the suffixes.
- Show Me: discuss the meaning of *maisonette* (French) and *sapling*.
- Identify prefixes mini and micro in the same way.
- Get Up and Go: ask individuals to ring the root words.
- Then look for other adjectives on the page: *pygmy, reduced, tiny, petite, baby, junior*.
- Point out that adding y often indicates smallness: *babe – baby, doll – dolly, pup – puppy*. Do the children know any other 'baby talk' words meaning 'small'? (e.g. *teeny weeny*)
- Introduce the oddbod: *under* – see below.

Pupil activities
A: Identify prefixes and suffixes meaning 'small'.
B: Add mini, ling, ette and micro to roots to make new words.
C: Find words with mini, micro.

Extra challenge: Find the meaning of *nanosecond*.

Review
- Recap the different prefixes and suffixes meaning 'small'.
- Have they found prefixes for 'large'? Elicit maxi, macro, hyper, super, and examples of words, e.g. *maximum, maximise, macrocosm, supermarket*. There aren't any equivalent suffixes.

Homework
Collect words, prefixes and suffixes meaning 'large'.

Oddbod   under 💬
- What's the opposite of *under*? (*over*) Both have er at the end.
- Look at how *under* combines with other words (e.g. *understand, underscore*).
- Link to *thunder*.
- Make up a mnemonic: *unicorns never do eat roses*.

Snip-snap   Nickname Investigation 💬
- Brainstorm nicknames and diminutives ending in y or ie, e.g. *Jonesy, Bobby, Billy, Terry, Maggie, Chrissy, Susie, Twiggy, Froggy*.
- Sort them into alphabetical order.
- Work out the original names.
- How many change the initial letter? (e.g. *Robert – Bobby*)
- Discuss links with baby talk and endearments, e.g. *poppet, darling, ducky*.

NLS objective for Unit 18

4.3.W12

Part 2 | **You need** | Big Book page 37; dry-wipe boards or notebooks

Whole class
- Before looking at the BBk, check homework. Draw out spelling points, e.g. ic and ous endings in *terrific, enormous*.
- Then turn to the BBk page. Look at the words and ask children to sort them into synonyms for *small* and *big*. Look at *infinitesimal* and identify the root (*infinite*) and the meaning ('immeasurable').
- Explain the derivation of *Lilliputian* (from Swift's *Gulliver's Travels*).
- Then look at the synonyms for *big*. Elicit or point out derivations, e.g. *gigantic* from *giant*; *titanic* from *titan*.
- Identify slang or invented words, e.g. *ginormous, humongous*.
- Can children spot any prefixes meaning 'small'? (mini, micro) Identify the prefix ultra, meaning 'extremely'.
- Compose a short shared text with contrasting phrases describing a tiny Tom Thumb and a towering giant: *tiny little mannikin / measureless monster*.

Review
- Read some of the contrasting phrases.
- Homework review.
- Sum up the various findings from homework and independent work by deciding how you might display the collections in the classroom – maybe small words could be made into a miniature book and large words into a huge poster.

Follow-up homework
Oddbod roundup: write a story using the term's oddbods.

Test dictation
- OB I'm wearing a suitable miniskirt under my coat.
- A   The boys sat sleepily in the back of the minibus.
      The leaflet described the important new invention.
- B   A gosling, a kitten and a puppy are all baby animals.
      That microscope is not suitable for children.
- C   The class was working with minimum supervision.

Snip-snap   Make-your-own Diminutives
- Write up diminutive add-ons, e.g. mini, ling, let.
- In pairs, children invent new diminutives using prefixes or suffixes, writing them on dry-wipe boards with their definitions, e.g. *lessonette – a very short lesson*.
- Pairs read out their new words and others guess the definitions.
- If necessary, provide some roots as well, e.g. *lesson, lunch, bike, bee, snack, magazine, mobile phone*.

Snip-snap   Key Word Roundup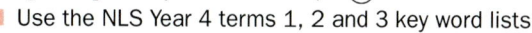
- Use the NLS Year 4 terms 1, 2 and 3 key word lists.
- Pairs start to work through the list, testing each other.
- Pairs write words correctly spelt in one list, problems in another.
- Continue until pairs have achieved ten correct spellings.
- Look at the words which cause the most problems and brainstorm strategies.

A1 Spelling strategies

> ### Objectives for Additional Unit 1
> To identify mis-spelt words and develop spelling strategies

Part 1 **You need** Big Book page 38; dry-wipe boards or notebooks; Pupil's Book pages 38–39; PCM A1

Whole class
- Tell the children that you are going to be talking about tricky words and common spelling errors.
- Focus on the BBk page. Explain the meaning of *error analysis* – working out why something is wrong.
- Look at the examples Blake has already completed.
- Point out that there are several different reasons for spelling errors: not hearing all the parts of a word, mixing up sounds, not remembering a rule, spelling it as it sounds, getting letters in the wrong order.
- Take each word, work out what has caused the mistake and decide what strategy will help. For example: *trys* – y to ie rule – revise the rule; *dissappear* – prefix rule: just add to word – more practice, learn with *disagree*; *haveing* – dropping e when adding ing rule – revise the rule, list examples: *loving*, *shining*; *evry* – not hearing all the written letters pronounced – link with *ever*.
- Point out that spelling involves **eye**, **ear**, **hand** and **brain**. People are sometimes better at using one than another. Brainstorm different strategies that the children employ.
- Introduce the oddbod: *other* – see below.

Pupil activities
A: Analyse four errors.
B: Analyse five errors and find another word with the same pattern.
C: Analyse six errors and find other words with the same pattern.

Think about ...: Which kind of error do you make most?

Review
- Recap the purpose of error analysis – if you know why you've made a mistake, then you're in a better position to put it right.
- Ask anyone who has thought about ear, eye, hand and brain distinctions in their own errors to share their findings.
- Introduce homework by emphasising that everyone has words that bug them and everyone has different ways of remembering tricky words.

Homework Spelling questionnaire.

Oddbod other
- Link it to *mother* and *brother*.
- Focus on the unusual pronunciation of o (although there's some regional variation – see the Snip-snap on the right).

Snip-snap Regional Differences
- Point out that not everyone speaks in the same way.
- Explore variations, e.g. *book* with 'long' **oo** as in *room*; *after* with 'short' **a**; *bath* to rhyme with *hearth*.
- Accent sometimes makes spelling patterns easier, e.g. 'short' **a** in *after* doesn't mislead you into hearing **ar**.
- Sometimes accent makes it harder, e.g. some pronunciations of *everything* can mislead you into hearing it as *evrythink*.
- Start a collection of words pronounced differently in your class or locality.

> ### NLS objectives for Additional Unit 1
> 4.3.W1   4.3.W2   4.3.W3

Part 2 | You need   Big Book page 39; dry-wipe boards or notebooks

Whole class
- Focus on the BBk page. Ask children to read the speech bubbles aloud.
- Discuss each one in turn, making sure you cover the following points:
  – *I'm really worried about making a mistake, so I use easy words.* You get to be a better speller by taking risks and having a go.
  – *If I don't know how to spell a word, how can I look it up in the dictionary?* Do it step by step. You can generally work out the initial letter or its alternatives, then think of likely vowel sound spellings.
  – *If I don't know a spelling I write it out in different ways and go for the one that looks right.* Remind the children again that spelling depends on eye, ear, hand and brain. Refer to inside back cover of the BBk.
  – *Learning words with a spelling partner has really helped me.* Working with somebody else can give you confidence, help you to concentrate, share problems.
- Which techniques do they use, and which one helps them most?

Review
- Sum up by brainstorming spelling strategies (see page 16 of the PCM Book).
- Revisit the icons on the inside back cover of the BBk.

- Homework review.
- Discuss children's findings and make a poster with class spelling resolutions.

Follow-up homework
Think of six words that you find tricky and decide which strategy will help you to remember each one.

Test dictation
OB   We played a football team from the other division.
A   The brothers were having a terrible fight.
     The duckling was loving its big adventure.
B   Mum shopped for hours and bought a new microwave.
     Ann dropped the doll out of the window into the garden below.
C   The wizard was full of mystery and tricks.

Snip-snap   Swap Shop
- In pairs, children swap books and identify words spelt incorrectly.
- Encourage them to identify the difficulty as precisely as possible.
- Establish a way of remembering the word, e.g. *friend* – i before e rule or mnemonic: *At the end I have a friend*.
- Finally, **Look Say Cover Write Check**.

Snip-snap   Key Word Sort
- Select a set of about five irregular tricky words from the Year 4 key word list, or ask children to select words they find difficult.
- In pairs, sort according to the 'tricky bits' – an unusual pronunciation (e.g. *don't*), an odd letter string (e.g. *through*).
- Practise suitable strategies, e.g. 'taking its photograph', drawing its outline, or saying the sounds separately as you write the word (e.g. *Wed-nes-day*) to emphasise the sounds you don't normally hear.

Making adjectives

Objective for Additional Unit 2

To use a range of suffixes to make adjectives and investigate spelling patterns

Part 1

You need   Big Book page 40; dry-wipe boards or notebooks; Pupil's Book pages 40–41; PCM A2

Whole class
- Remind the children of previous work on adding suffixes to change words, e.g. adding *ness* can change an adjective into a noun, e.g. *kind – kindness*.
- Explain that today you're looking at making adjectives out of nouns and verbs.
- Focus on the BBk page. Point out how useful it is to be able to make new words out of bits and pieces – a word recycling factory.
- Look at the nouns and verbs which go into the recycling factory.
- Get Up and Go: ask volunteers to join the nouns and verbs to the recycled adjectives.
- Identify the different suffixes and write them in the 'suffixes box' (*ic*, *able*, *ish*, *y*, *ful*).
- Challenge the children to find some more adjectives with these endings, e.g. *poetic, manageable, selfish, stressful*.
- Look more closely at the way some of the words change, e.g. *manage* keeps the final *e*; *sarcasm* changes *m* to *tic*.
- Revise different parts of speech (verb, noun, adjective), e.g. *enjoy – enjoyment – enjoyable*.
- Look at which nouns can be transformed into verbs and which can't, e.g. there's no verb from *child* or *sarcasm*.
- Compose a sentence using the noun, verb and adjective in the same sentence, e.g. *I felt apologetic so I apologised, but he wouldn't accept my apology*.
- Point out that there are several other suffixes you can add to make adjectives – group C will be looking for some new ones.
- Introduce the oddbod: *electricity* – see below.

Pupil activities
A: Match words and suffixes to make adjectives.
B: Make nouns into adjectives and find verbs with the same roots.
C: Sort nouns and verbs, then make adjectives.

Extra challenge: Make three adjectives from *terror*.

Review
- Ask group C to contribute new suffixes to the collection.
- Look at the adjectives made in the Extra challenge: *terrifying, terrible, terrific*.
- Remind the children of the different parts of speech and make sentences.
- Demonstrate how to turn an adjective into a noun, e.g. *stupid – stupidity*.

Homework   Sort root words into those that will change before adding an adjective suffix and those that won't.

Oddbod   electricity
- Identify the *ity* suffix.
- Say the adjective *electric* out loud.
- Note other science vocabulary using the same root, e.g. *electrical*, another adjective.
- Note the hard and soft *c*.
- Demonstrate handwriting joins and practise on dry-wipe boards.

Snip-snap   Verb, Noun, Adjective
- Write headings on the board: *verb, noun, adjective*.
- Write some verbs in the first column, e.g. *play, enjoy, hope, wish, threaten*.
- Children race to supply words for the remaining columns.
- Watch out for catch-you-outs where verb and noun are the same.

NLS objectives for Additional Unit 2
4.3.W3   4.3.W8

Part 2 | **You need**   Big Book page 41; dry-wipe boards or notebooks

Whole class
- Focus on the BBk page. Read the passage together.
- Establish that the words in brackets need to be turned into adjectives by adding a suffix.
- Brainstorm the suffixes the children have come across already and make a list on the board, e.g. ful, able, ing, y, ish, some, ic, al, ous, ent, ant, ive.
- Time Out / Show Me: children try out adjectives on dry-wipe boards.
- Read the finished passage through again.
- Cross off the suffixes used in the passage from your list.
- Compose another sentence with any remaining suffixes from your list, e.g. *Our earth is smallish compared to the whole universe. It makes me feel quite nervous. It doesn't seem possible to survive.*

Review
- Help children to distinguish between adverbs and adjectives with ly endings and verbs and adjectives with ing endings by composing sentences, e.g. *He told me some shocking news while we were walking slowly to school.*
- Homework review.
- Look at the homework examples.
- Discuss the Extra challenge, making adjectives from nouns by adding ly, some or al.

Follow-up homework
Scan newspapers, magazines and books for examples of suffixes; sort the words into nouns, verbs and adjectives.

Test dictation
OB Many inventions use electricity.
A   Jen's new microscope is more powerful than her old one.
    Mum's ring is valuable and beautiful too.
B   Dad put the kettle on to make a refreshing drink.
    Greedy Jim began to sulk as there was no cake left.
C   Joe watched the suspicious man walking through the park.

Snip-snap   s or z Investigation 👁 💬
- Write a verb ending in ise on the board, e.g. *apologise.*
- Then write *apologize*. Which is right?
- Ask the children to check in dictionaries / spell checkers.
- Establish that it can be spelled either way; in America, ize is more common.
- Collect other examples, e.g. *realis/ze, economis/ze.*
- Find some exceptions, e.g. *surprise, compromise.*
- Investigate other endings, e.g. *isation*: does the same apply?

Snip-snap   Some Compounds 💬
- Write the word *some* on the board.
- In pairs, children find as many compounds as they can, using dictionaries, e.g. *sometimes, something, somewhere, somehow, somebody, someone, someday, someplace, somewhat, somewhen.*
- Discuss meanings and distinguish the colloquialisms *someplace, somewhen.*
- Do the same with *earth, eye, half* (look at hyphens, e.g. *half-term*).

A3 Contractions

Objectives for Additional Unit 3

To revise common contractions; to distinguish the two forms *its* and *it's* and to use these accurately in own writing

Part 1

You need Big Book page 42, dry-wipe boards or notebooks;
Pupil's Book pages 42–43; PCM A3

Whole class
- Write the word *I'm* on the board.
- Ask the children what it means, then write out in full: *I am*.
- Remind the children of Year 3 work (see Unit 10).
- Introduce the term *contraction* – making something smaller or shorter.
- Explain that you make the word shorter by cutting out a letter. You show where the letter was by putting in an *apostrophe*.
- Focus on the BBk page. Help the children to work out how the 'short cut box' works.
- Ask volunteers to fill in the blank boxes.
- Time Out: children use dry-wipe boards to draw a box and fill.
- Point out that contractions are generally used in informal writing, e.g. dialogue in stories.
- Read the dialogue on the page, commenting particularly on *won't*, where the original word *will* changes.
- Continue with the dialogue; include an example of an apostrophe showing possession and briefly revise this use. Make sure children are aware of the difference between *its* (possession) and *it's* (*it is*).
- Introduce the oddbod: *don't* – see below.

Pupil activities
A: Change dialogue to contractions.
B: Write out contractions in full and compose a dialogue using contractions.
C: Sort apostrophes into contractions and possession and continue dialogue.

Extra challenge: Make a reminder card for *its* and *it's*.

Review
- Read some of the dialogue examples.
- Ask group C children to give an example of an apostrophe showing belonging.
- Focus on *it's* and *its*. Teach the following mnemonic: <u>*It's*</u> *really hard to remember apostrophes. When you leave out a letter or letters, you put an apostrophe in* <u>*its*</u> *place.*

Homework Make contractions cards to play *Snap* or *Pelmanism*.

Oddbod don't
- This word behaves regularly apart from its misleading pronunciation.
- Learn it with other contractions and the rhyming pair *won't*, which is unusual because the base words change: *will not – won't*.

Snip-snap Contraction Snap
- Use the Contraction Snap cards from homework.
- In pairs, children play *Snap* in the traditional manner.
- At the end of the game, pairs test each other on spelling the contractions.

NLS objective for Additional Unit 3
4.3.W10

Part 2

You need Big Book page 43; dry-wipe boards or notebooks; marker pen; very small 'dot' type sticky labels

Whole class
- Remind the children of Year 3 work (see Unit 10).
- Focus on the BBk page. Let children spot the deliberate mistakes.
- Get Up and Go: children put the apostrophes in the right place, and explain how the word has been shortened: *don't/do not; I'm/I am; it's/it is* in *It's a bargain* and *it's the juiciest; you'll/you will; you'd/you had*.
- Help out with *o'clock* (*of the clock*), which may not be familiar.
- Ask the children to spot the apostrophes that shouldn't be there (*carrot's, pear's*) and to explain why not; cover the apostrophe with a sticky dot.
- Discuss the reason for people making the *carrot's* and *pear's* mistake – confusing plural s with apostrophe s signifying 'belonging to'.
- Read the shop name together – *Murray's Stores*. Distinguish between plural s as in *stores* and possessive s meaning 'belonging to Murray'.
- Point out that a lot of adults get apostrophes wrong. Sometimes they scatter them everywhere and sometimes they leave them out.

Review
- Recap the use of apostrophes to show where letters are missing in contractions.
- Briefly remind the children of the use of apostrophes to show belonging.
- Ask the children to provide an example of each kind of apostrophe.

- Homework review.
- Check that children completed the cards correctly, and, if time, allow a few minutes for them to play *Snap* or *Pelmanism* in pairs.

Follow-up homework
Look in books, magazines, newspapers and notices to find as many examples of apostrophes as you can.

Test dictation
OB Don't stay awake too late at night.
A You've been very energetic this morning.
I've stopped being silly at school.
B I think we've rested for long enough now.
He'll have to overtake that car if he wants to win.
C You mustn't postpone doing your homework.

Snip-snap Short Cuts 👁 ✍
- Use the idea on the BBk page for a quick-fire session.
- Draw boxes on board with the full version in place, e.g. *could not.*
- Ask volunteers to fill in the 'short cut' contraction.
- Vary by filling in the contraction and asking volunteers to provide the full version.
- Children could set a challenge for their partner.

Snip-snap Key Word Sentence Race 💬
- Make a set of cards from the key word list.
- Give pairs of children four cards each.
- Children race to compose a sentence using all the words.
- The winning pair says the sentence and spells the key words.

Facsimile Big Book pages

This section contains facsimiles of the Big Book pages for ease of planning.

1 Double consonants

Part 1

Sort these words into two lists.

below   diner   hopping   written   taping
super   rider   coma   pined   pollen
supper   hoping   writing   comma
bellow   dinner   ridding   tapping
pinned   pole   dinner   comma
stopped

Part 2

Complete the lines using rhyming couplets.

Dr Foster

Dr Foster sent a letter
All his patients felt much better.
Dr Foster changed a
Now the baby feels quite
Dr Foster wore a
It only cost him half a
Dr Foster thought it
To hop around just like a
Dr Foster took up
He knows the exercise is
Dr Foster kept a
All it wanted was a

carrot	happy	funny	collar	swimming
bunny	slimming	parrot	nappy	dollar

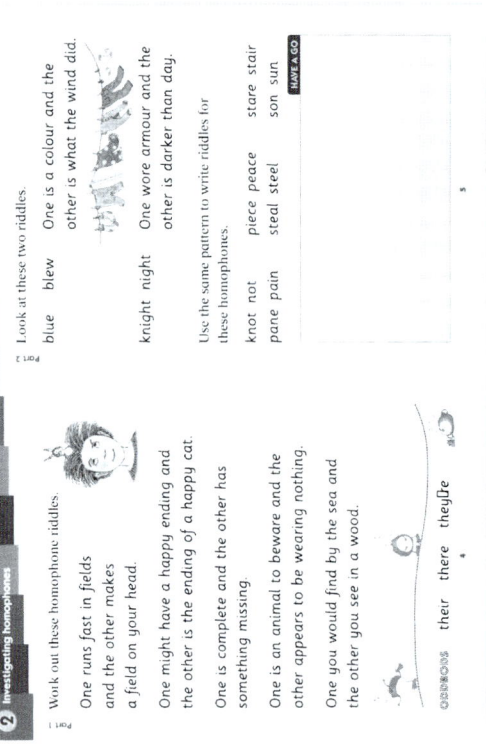

2 Investigating homophones

Part 1

Work out these homophonic riddles.

One runs fast in fields
and the other makes
a field on your head.

One might have a happy ending and
the other is the ending of a happy cat.

One is complete and the other has
something missing.

One is an animal to beware and the
other appears to be wearing nothing.

One you would find by the sea and
the other you see in a wood.

their   there   they're

Part 2

Look at these two riddles.

blue   blew   One is a colour and the
other is what the wind did.

knight   night   One wore armour and the
other is darker than day.

Use the same pattern to write riddles for
these homophones.

knot   not   piece   peace   stare   stair
pane   pain   steal   steel   son   sun

HAVE A GO

3 Verb endings

Part 1

Write the verb and different verb endings
for each picture.

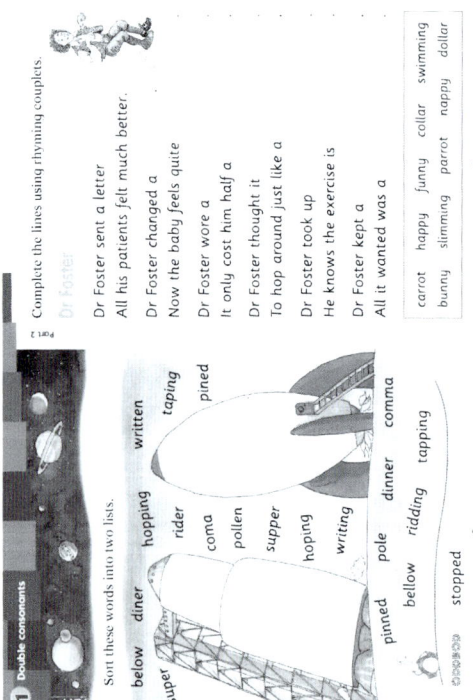

asked

HAVE A GO

Part 2

Complete the chart.

verb	+ s	+ ing	+ ed
help ask look	helps asks	helping looking	helped
hope stare smile	hopes	staring	stared
slip pat bet	slips		slipped
rush dress box		dressing boxing	rushed
carry try play	plays	carrying	

4 Irregular tense changes

Part 1

Correct the baby talk.
Circle the past tense verbs
that are not right.

I goed to the party.

Daddy bringed me my toys.

I finded my shoes.

I knowed my way home.

I telled my teddy off for being silly.

My brother leaved me alone.

I weared my new shoes.

I catched a ball when Grandad throwed it.

think   thought

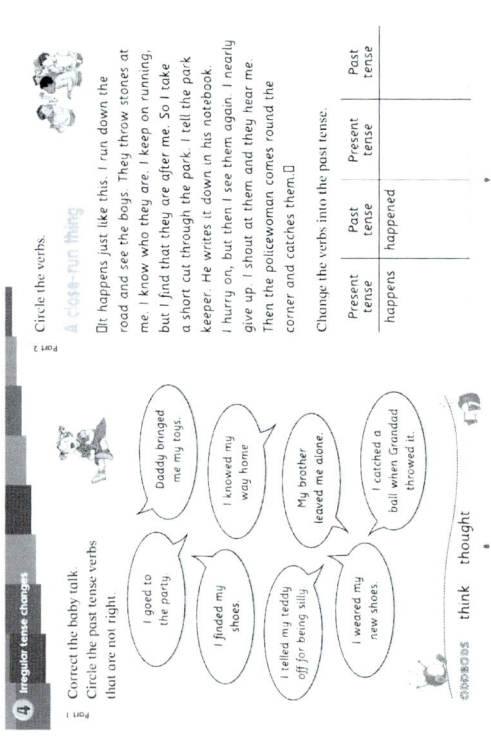

Part 2

Circle the verbs.

A cross-run thing

It happens just like this. I run down the
road and see the boys. They throw stones at
me. I know who they are. I keep on running,
but I find that they are after me. So I take
a short cut through the park. I tell the park
keeper. He writes it down in his notebook.
I hurry on, but then I see them again. I nearly
give up. I shout at them and they hear me.
Then the policewoman comes round the
corner and catches them.

Change the verbs into the past tense:

Present tense	Past tense	Present tense	Past tense
happens	happened		

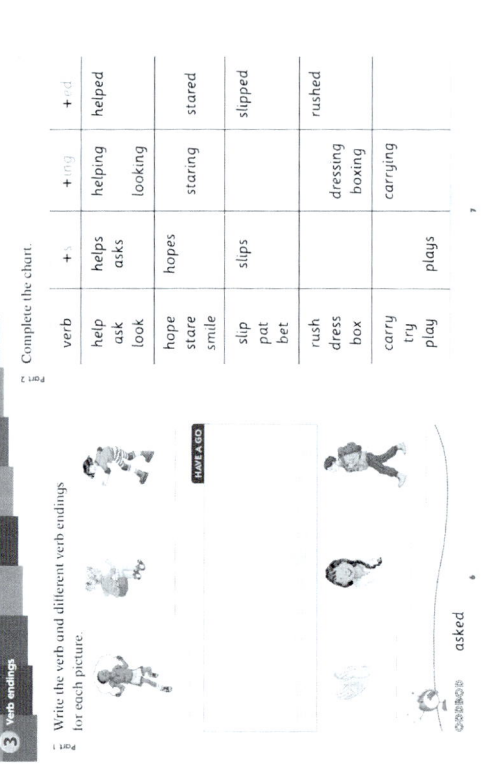

Facsimile Big Book pages cont.

Part 1

5 Suffixes: *al*, *ing* and *ic*

My Pal

My pal
Is acrobatic –
She can touch her nose
With her tongue and her toes.

My pal
Is atomic –
She is faster than light
As she flies through the night.

My pal
Is exceptional,
She juggles with jelly
While she watches the telly.

My pal
Is a rhythmic,
Heart-beating,
Foot-tapping,
Thigh-slapping,
Cool-rapping,
Word-rapping,
Poet!

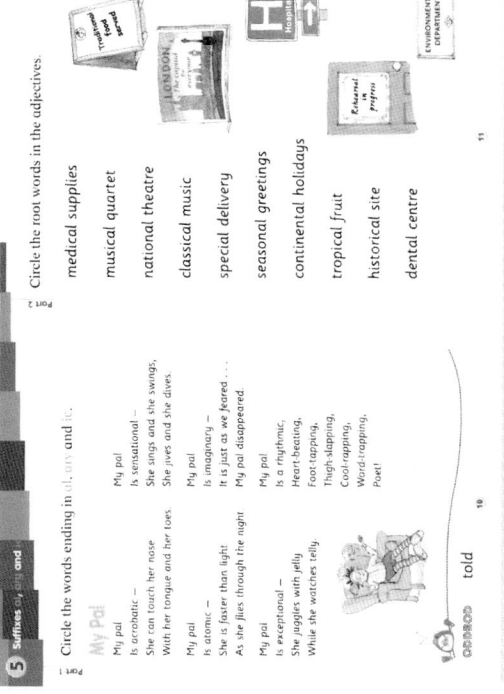

being

Part 2

Circle the root words in the adjectives.

medical supplies
musical quartet
national theatre
classical music
special delivery
seasonal greetings
continental holidays
tropical fruit
historical site
dental centre

told

6 Using suffixes to change word class

Part 1

1. Pick a word
2. Add a suffix.
3. Make a verb.

nouns + adjectives in
suffixes in
verbs out
lengthen

standard, horror, elastic, note, flat, medium, thick, straight, apology

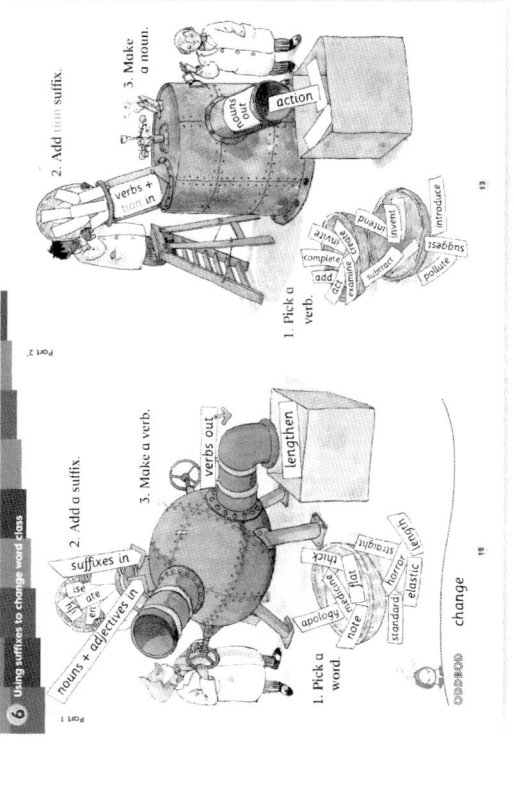

change

Part 2

1. Pick a verb.
2. Add *tion* suffix.
3. Make a noun.

verbs + *tion* in
nouns out
action

complete, examine, invite, intend, introduce, frustrate, add, pollute, invent

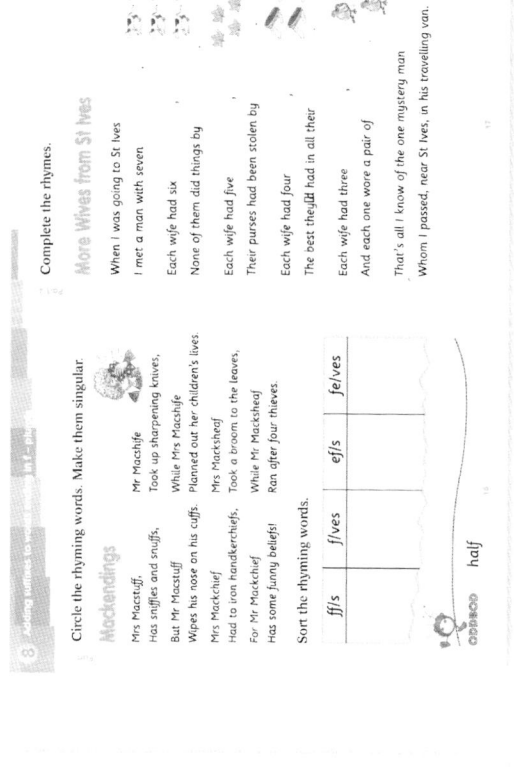

7 adding suffixes

Write some more verses for the Loch Ness Rap.

The Loch Ness Rap

What's that shape
Moving in the lake?
Caught it on my camera
Make no mistake.

Dreadful ugliness,
Greyness, shabbiness.
Chorus

Swims with gracefulness,
Sings with tunefulness!
Chorus

Watch with helplessness,
See its fearlessness.
Chorus

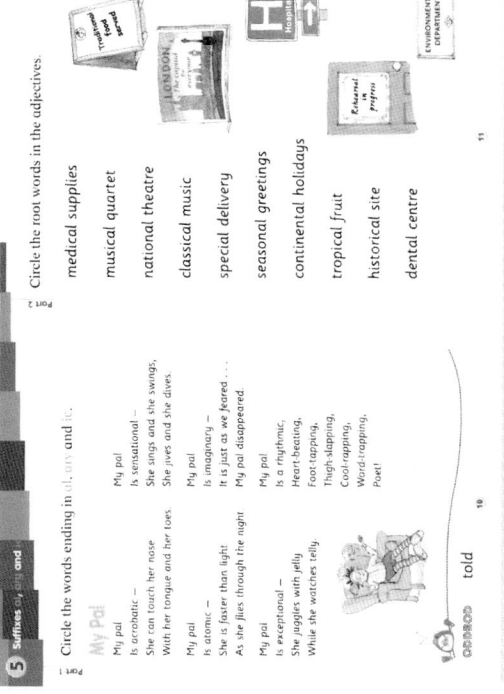

Complete the words in brackets with the correct suffix.

dom   ish   some   ment   ness   ship   hood

A wise king

Once upon a time, in a distant (king) lived a (hand) king who had been known for his (wise) and (cheerful) since his (child). All the people had their (free) and they lived in (friend) with each other, working in (partner).

One day, four wild tigers came to the (king). They were the most (fierce). (loathe) and (meddle) animals.

The chief (govern) adviser said to the king, 'D'your (High), we are being attacked by a (trouble) menace What shall we do?'

The king said that they should rid the country of the (fiend) Jour Dit is (fool) to allow them to destroy our people's (happy) and (enjoy),' he declared.

8 adding suffixes to words ending in *f*, *fe*

Circle the rhyming words. Make them singular.

Mockendings

Mrs Macstuff
Has sniffles and snuffs,
But Mr Macstuff
Wipes his nose on his cuffs.

Mrs Mackshef
Had to iron handkerchiefs,
For Mr Mackshef
Has some funny beliefs!

Mr Machife
Took up sharpening knives,
While Mrs Machife
Planned out her children's lives.

Mrs Mackshef
Took a broom to the leaves,
While Mr Mackshef
Ran after four thieves.

Sort the rhyming words.

ff/s	f/ves	ef/s	fe/ves

half

More Wives from St Ives

Complete the rhymes.

When I was going to St Ives
I met a man with seven

Each wife had six
None of them did things by

Each wife had five
Their purses had been stolen by

Each wife had four
The best they'd had in all their

Each wife had three
And each one wore a pair of

That's all I know of the one mystery man
Whom I passed, near St Ives, in his travelling van.

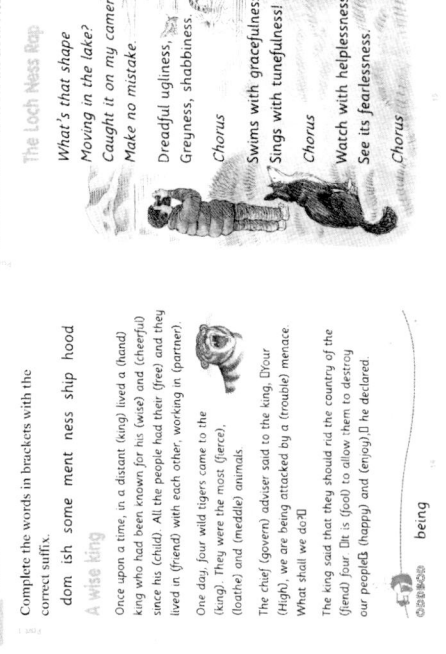

Facsimile Big Book pages cont.

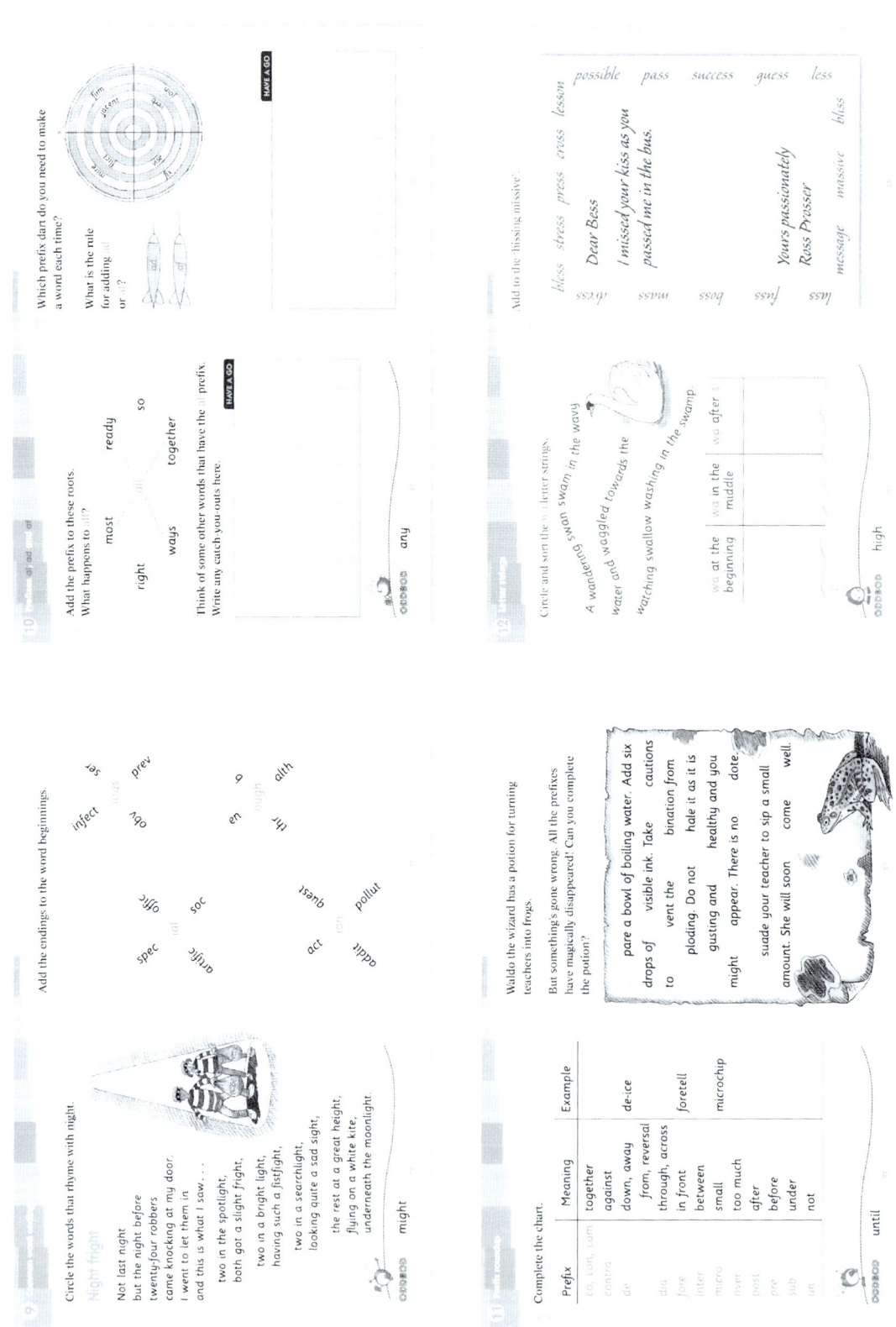

Night fright

Circle the words that rhyme with night.

Not last night
but the night before
twenty-four robbers
came knocking at my door.
I went to let them in
and this is what I saw. . . .

two in the spotlight,
both got a slight fright,

two in a bright light,
having such a fistfight,

two in a searchlight,
looking quite a sad sight,

the rest at a great height,
flying on a white kite,
underneath the moonlight.

might

Add the endings to the word beginnings.

infect
ser
prev
obv
spon
a
alth
en
thr
nutr
offic
soc
spec
artific
act
quest
vuln
addic
pollut

Complete the chart.

Prefix	Meaning	Example
co, con, com	together	
contra	against	
de	down, away	de-ice
dis	from, reversal	
trans	through, across	
fore	in front	foretell
inter	between	
micro	small	microchip
over	too much	
post	after	
pre	before	
sub	under	
un	not	

until

Waldo the wizard has a potion for turning
teachers into frogs.

But something's gone wrong. All the prefixes
have magically disappeared! Can you complete
the potion?

pare a bowl of boiling water. Add six
drops of   visible ink. Take   cautions
to   vent the   bination from
      ploding. Do not   hale it as it is
      gusting and   healthy and you
might   appear. There is no   dote.
      suade your teacher to sip a small
amount. She will soon   come   well.

Which prefix darn do you need to make
a word each time?

firm
green
ject
fit
must
go
take
blue

What is the rule
for adding al
or il?

Add the prefix to these roots.
What happens to all?

most   ready
right   all   so
ways   together

HAVE A GO

Think of some other words that have the all prefix.
Write any catch you-outs here.

any

Add to the hissing missive.

bliss   stress   press   cross   lessn
possible   pass   success   guess   less

dress   mass   boss   fuss   less
less   boss   fuss   less

Dear Bess
I missed your kiss as you
passed me in the bus.

Yours passionately
Ross Prasser

message   massive   bliss

Circle and sort the wa letter strings.

A wandering swan swam in the wavy
water and waggled towards the
watching swallow washing in the swamp.

wa at the beginning	wa in the middle	wa after s

high

Facsimile Big Book pages cont.

13 Investigating c and k

Part 1

Investigate kicking k in words.

Beginning	Middle	End
kick	tickle	back
kite	take	kick
kiss	ankle	sink
kill	shake	talk
king	crackle	bark
kitchen	broken	trick

across

Part 2

Investigate the consonant v and write some rules below.

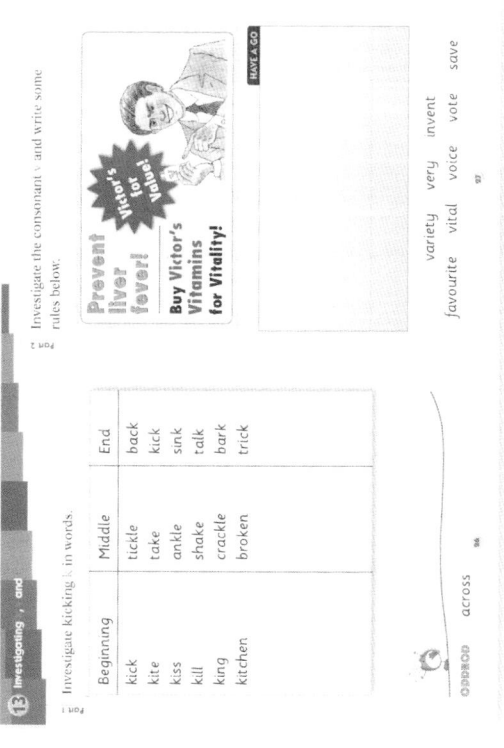

Prevent liver fever!
Buy Victor's Vitamins for Vitality!
Victor's for Value!

HAVE A GO

favourite   very   invent
variety   vital   voice   vote   save

14 Same spelling, different pronunciation

Part 1

Circle pairs or groups of matching letter strings.

The Chaos

Dearest creature in creation,
Studying English pronunciation,
I will teach you in my verse
Sounds like corpse, corps, horse and worse.
It will keep you Susy, busy,
Make your head with heat grow dizzy;
Tear in eye, your dress you'll tear;
So shall I! Oh, hear my prayer,
Pray, console your loving poet.
Make my coat look new, dear, sew it!
Just compare heart, beard and heard;
Dies and diet; lord and word;
River, rival; tomb and comb;
Doll and roll and some and home!

though

Part 2

Circle the pairs of non-rhymes with matching letter strings.

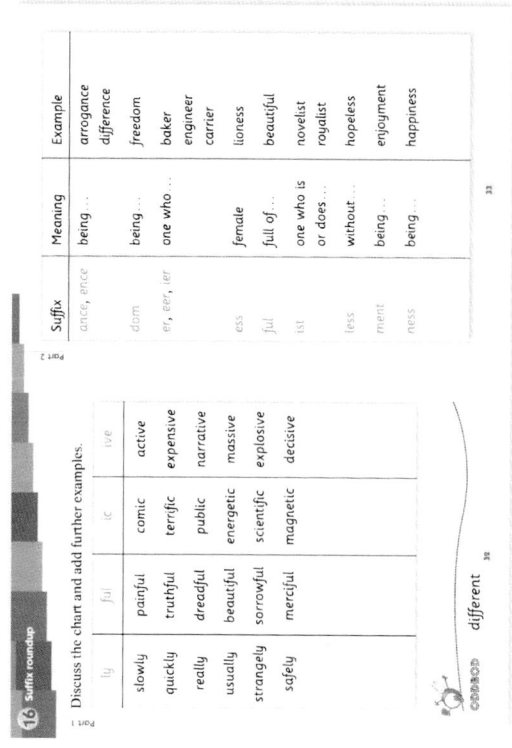

Let me see the wound. It's bound to hurt.

His bone has gone! What have you done with it?

Watch me play catch!

Get to work with this fork.

I've gone through enough!

15 Common roots

Part 1

Circle the roots. Can you guess what the roots mean?

predict	phone
dictation	microphone
dictionary	xylophone
dictate	phoneme
verdict	telephone
dictator	

press	port
impress	transport
pressure	import
depress	export
express	porter
repress	deport

sure

Part 2

Trace the word web for telephone. Try to add to it.

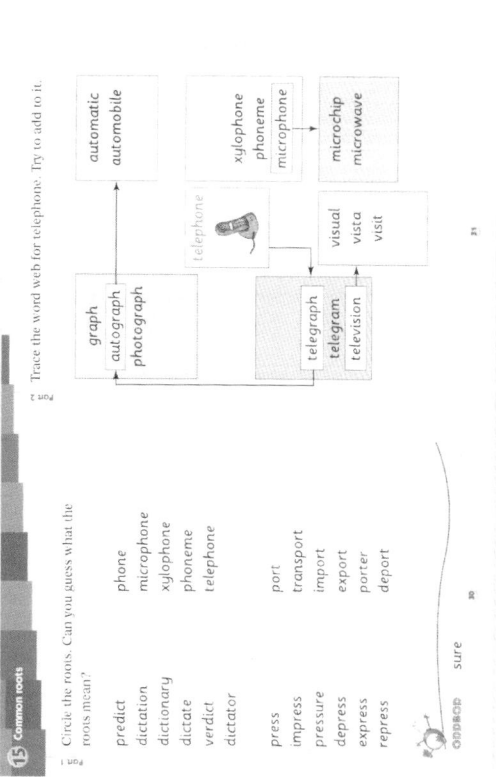

graph — autograph, photograph
telephone
automatic, automobile
xylophone, phoneme, microphone
telegraph, telegram, television
visual, vista, visit
microchip, microwave

16 Suffix roundup

Part 1

Discuss the chart and add further examples.

ly	ful	ic	ive
slowly	painful	comic	active
quickly	truthful	terrific	expensive
really	dreadful	public	narrative
usually	beautiful	energetic	massive
strangely	sorrowful	scientific	explosive
safely	merciful	magnetic	decisive

different

Part 2

Suffix	Meaning	Example
ance, ence	being ...	arrogance, difference
dom	being ...	freedom
er, eer, ier	one who ...	baker, engineer, carrier
ess	female	lioness
ful	full of ...	beautiful
ist	one who is or does ...	novelist, royalist
less	without ...	hopeless
ment	being ...	enjoyment
ness	being ...	happiness

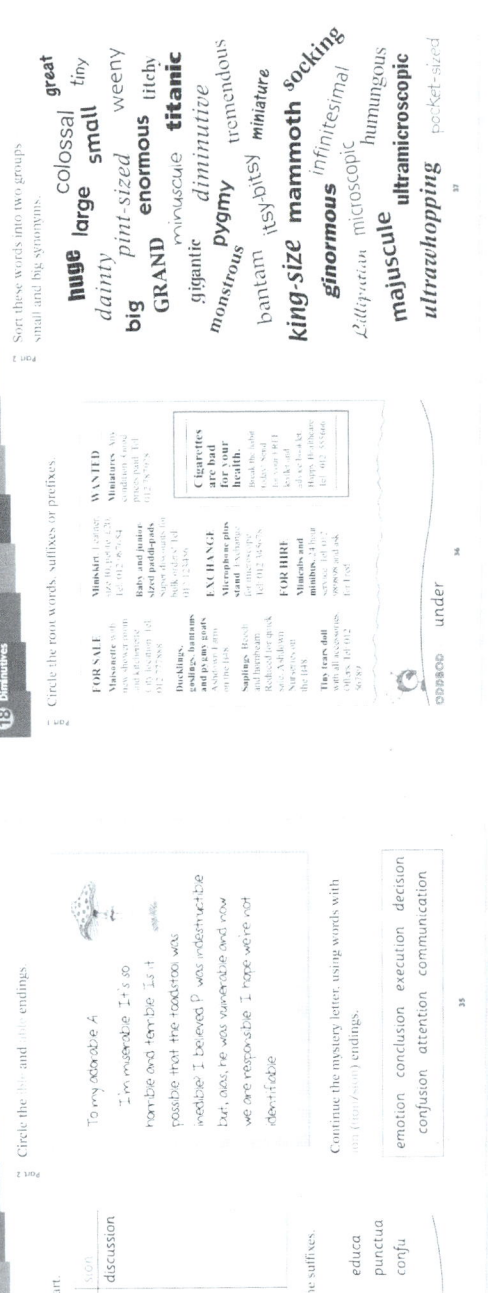
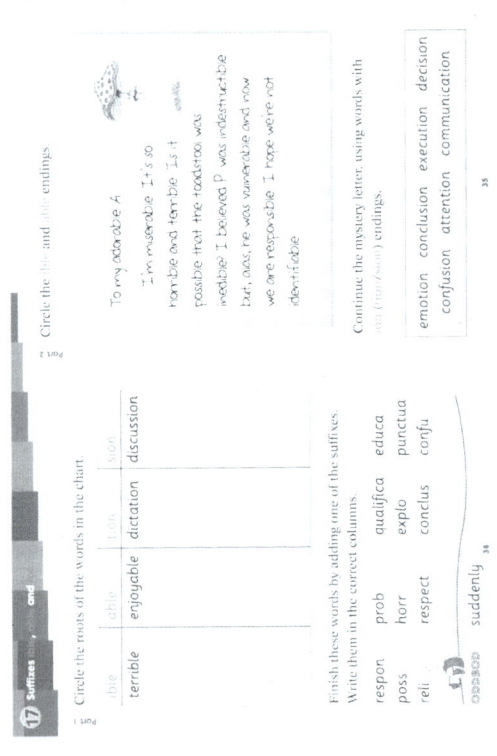

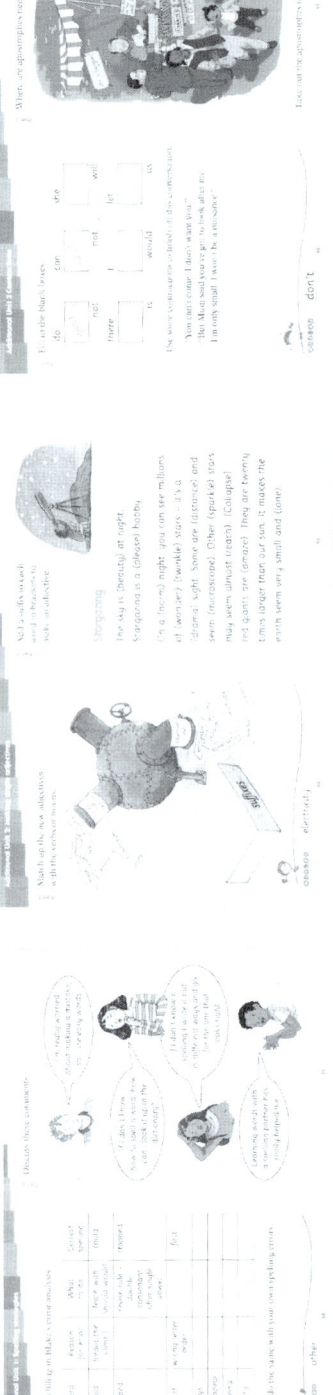